Family History Record Book

AN EIGHT-GENERATION FAMILY TREE WORKBOOK TO RECORD YOUR RESEARCH

heritagehunter

Find other history publications at
www.heritagehunter.co.uk

ISBN 978-1-905315-31-4 (paperback)
ISBN 978-1-905315-32-1 (hardback)

Sign up for the free Histories newsletter at
www.gethistories.com

How to use this book

Keeping track of your family history can soon get tricky as the amount of information you gather about each ancestor builds up. This book provides you with an easy way to keep all of this information in one place – this makes it ideal for a summary of your research which you can carry with you if you are visiting archives and libraries, and indeed a great way to share your family history with relatives for posterity.

The book has two main sections. The first, covering pages iv to xxi, provides an opportunity to record an at-a-glance summary of your direct ancestors. Pages iv and v cover four generations – ie from yourself (or whoever your starting individual is) back to your great-grandparents. Then each of those great-grandparents has their own double-page spread where you can record four more generations of their ancestors.

You'll see that every single person in your tree of ancestors has been allocated a number, shown in bold – this is known in genealogy as an Ahnentafel number (see https://www.thoughtco.com/ahnentafel-numbering-system-explained-1420744, for example). It's very simple to use: to find any person's father, simply double their number – and to find their mother, double it and add one. Or, of course, conversely, you can go down the generations by halving (take away one from an add number first). This means that all even numbers represent male ancestors, and odd numbers female ones (number 1 is reserved for you or any other starting individual, and can be either male or female). Male ancestors are also indicated with a gray tint.

So the second part of this book allocates half a page to each of your 254 forebears going back to the eighth generation (where you count as the first). You can sue the bold numbers to find an individual quickly, and of course all this cross-references with the summary pages in the first part of the book. And these numbers cover the overall generations:

Parents	2–3
Grandparents	4–7
Great-grandparents	8–15
2x-great-grandparents	16–31
3x-great-grandparents	32–63
4x-great-grandparents	64–127
5x-great-grandparents	128–255

For each individual, you can note down your key pieces of information, organised by date, the source of the information (eg census, parish record, specific archive, etc) and the actual details – there's room for up to 16 items per person, and of course these can include anything from vital dates to occupations, children born or where they lived.

If you have exhausted the standard types of record, and you are researching ancestors from England, Scotland, Ireland or Wales, do also take a look at the timeline chart at the back of the book. This is a very useful summary of more than 100 different sources organised by the time periods they cover. Also at the back is a useful cousin calculator.

GENERATIONS 1 TO 4

PARENTS

2	Name: B: / / M: / / D: / / Occupation: Notes:

SELF

1	Name: B: / / M: / / D: / / Occupation: Notes:

3	Name: B: / / M: / / D: / / Occupation: Notes:

GRANDPARENTS

4 Name:
B: / / M: / / D: / /
Occupation:
Notes:

5 Name:
B: / / M: / / D: / /
Occupation:
Notes:

6 Name:
B: / / M: / / D: / /
Occupation:
Notes:

7 Name:
B: / / M: / / D: / /
Occupation:
Notes:

8 Name:
B: / / M: / / D: / /
Occupation:
Notes:

GO TO **vi**

9 Name:
B: / / M: / / D: / /
Occupation:
Notes:

GO TO **viii**

10 Name:
B: / / M: / / D: / /
Occupation:
Notes:

GO TO **x**

11 Name:
B: / / M: / / D: / /
Occupation:
Notes:

GO TO **xii**

12 Name:
B: / / M: / / D: / /
Occupation:
Notes:

GO TO **xiv**

13 Name:
B: / / M: / / D: / /
Occupation:
Notes:

GO TO **xvi**

14 Name:
B: / / M: / / D: / /
Occupation:
Notes:

GO TO **xviii**

15 Name:
B: / / M: / / D: / /
Occupation:
Notes:

GO TO **xx**

GENERATIONS 5 TO 8

(PATERNAL ANCESTORS)

GREAT-GREAT-GREAT-GRANDPARENTS

32 Name:
B: / / M: / / D: / /
Occupation:
Notes:

GREAT-GREAT-GRANDPARENTS

16 Name:
B: / / M: / / D: / /
Occupation:
Notes:

33 Name:
B: / / M: / / D: / /
Occupation:
Notes:

8

34 Name:
B: / / M: / / D: / /
Occupation:
Notes:

17 Name:
B: / / M: / / D: / /
Occupation:
Notes:

35 Name:
B: / / M: / / D: / /
Occupation:
Notes:

64 Name:
B: / / M: / / D: / /
Occupation:
Notes:

128 Name:
B: / / M: / / D: / /

129 Name:
B: / / M: / / D: / /

65 Name:
B: / / M: / / D: / /
Occupation:
Notes:

130 Name:
B: / / M: / / D: / /

131 Name:
B: / / M: / / D: / /

66 Name:
B: / / M: / / D: / /
Occupation:
Notes:

132 Name:
B: / / M: / / D: / /

133 Name:
B: / / M: / / D: / /

67 Name:
B: / / M: / / D: / /
Occupation:
Notes:

134 Name:
B: / / M: / / D: / /

135 Name:
B: / / M: / / D: / /

68 Name:
B: / / M: / / D: / /
Occupation:
Notes:

136 Name:
B: / / M: / / D: / /

137 Name:
B: / / M: / / D: / /

69 Name:
B: / / M: / / D: / /
Occupation:
Notes:

138 Name:
B: / / M: / / D: / /

139 Name:
B: / / M: / / D: / /

70 Name:
B: / / M: / / D: / /
Occupation:
Notes:

140 Name:
B: / / M: / / D: / /

141 Name:
B: / / M: / / D: / /

71 Name:
B: / / M: / / D: / /
Occupation:
Notes:

142 Name:
B: / / M: / / D: / /

143 Name:
B: / / M: / / D: / /

GENERATIONS 5 TO 8

(PATERNAL ANCESTORS)

GREAT-GREAT-GREAT-GRANDPARENTS

36 Name:
B: / / M: / / D: / /
Occupation:
Notes:

GREAT-GREAT-GRANDPARENTS

18 Name:
B: / / M: / / D: / /
Occupation:
Notes:

37 Name:
B: / / M: / / D: / /
Occupation:
Notes:

9

38 Name:
B: / / M: / / D: / /
Occupation:
Notes:

19 Name:
B: / / M: / / D: / /
Occupation:
Notes:

39 Name:
B: / / M: / / D: / /
Occupation:
Notes:

72 Name:
B: / / M: / / D: / /
Occupation:
Notes:

144 Name:
B: / / M: / / D: / /

145 Name:
B: / / M: / / D: / /

73 Name:
B: / / M: / / D: / /
Occupation:
Notes:

146 Name:
B: / / M: / / D: / /

147 Name:
B: / / M: / / D: / /

74 Name:
B: / / M: / / D: / /
Occupation:
Notes:

148 Name:
B: / / M: / / D: / /

149 Name:
B: / / M: / / D: / /

75 Name:
B: / / M: / / D: / /
Occupation:
Notes:

150 Name:
B: / / M: / / D: / /

151 Name:
B: / / M: / / D: / /

76 Name:
B: / / M: / / D: / /
Occupation:
Notes:

152 Name:
B: / / M: / / D: / /

153 Name:
B: / / M: / / D: / /

77 Name:
B: / / M: / / D: / /
Occupation:
Notes:

154 Name:
B: / / M: / / D: / /

155 Name:
B: / / M: / / D: / /

78 Name:
B: / / M: / / D: / /
Occupation:
Notes:

156 Name:
B: / / M: / / D: / /

157 Name:
B: / / M: / / D: / /

79 Name:
B: / / M: / / D: / /
Occupation:
Notes:

158 Name:
B: / / M: / / D: / /

159 Name:
B: / / M: / / D: / /

GENERATIONS 5 TO 8

(PATERNAL ANCESTORS)

GREAT-GREAT-GREAT-GRANDPARENTS

40 Name:

B: / / M: / / D: / /

Occupation:

Notes:

GREAT-GREAT-GRANDPARENTS

20 Name:

B: / / M: / / D: / /

Occupation:

Notes:

41 Name:

B: / / M: / / D: / /

Occupation:

Notes:

10

42 Name:

B: / / M: / / D: / /

Occupation:

Notes:

21 Name:

B: / / M: / / D: / /

Occupation:

Notes:

43 Name:

B: / / M: / / D: / /

Occupation:

Notes:

80 Name:
B: / / M: / / D: / /
Occupation:
Notes:

160 Name:
B: / / M: / / D: / /

161 Name:
B: / / M: / / D: / /

81 Name:
B: / / M: / / D: / /
Occupation:
Notes:

162 Name:
B: / / M: / / D: / /

163 Name:
B: / / M: / / D: / /

82 Name:
B: / / M: / / D: / /
Occupation:
Notes:

164 Name:
B: / / M: / / D: / /

165 Name:
B: / / M: / / D: / /

83 Name:
B: / / M: / / D: / /
Occupation:
Notes:

166 Name:
B: / / M: / / D: / /

167 Name:
B: / / M: / / D: / /

84 Name:
B: / / M: / / D: / /
Occupation:
Notes:

168 Name:
B: / / M: / / D: / /

169 Name:
B: / / M: / / D: / /

85 Name:
B: / / M: / / D: / /
Occupation:
Notes:

170 Name:
B: / / M: / / D: / /

171 Name:
B: / / M: / / D: / /

86 Name:
B: / / M: / / D: / /
Occupation:
Notes:

172 Name:
B: / / M: / / D: / /

173 Name:
B: / / M: / / D: / /

87 Name:
B: / / M: / / D: / /
Occupation:
Notes:

174 Name:
B: / / M: / / D: / /

175 Name:
B: / / M: / / D: / /

GENERATIONS 5 TO 8
(PATERNAL ANCESTORS)

GREAT-GREAT-GREAT-GRANDPARENTS

44 Name:
B: / / M: / / D: / /
Occupation:
Notes:

GREAT-GREAT-GRANDPARENTS

22 Name:
B: / / M: / / D: / /
Occupation:
Notes:

45 Name:
B: / / M: / / D: / /
Occupation:
Notes:

11

46 Name:
B: / / M: / / D: / /
Occupation:
Notes:

23 Name:
B: / / M: / / D: / /
Occupation:
Notes:

47 Name:
B: / / M: / / D: / /
Occupation:
Notes:

88 Name:
B: / / M: / / D: / /
Occupation:
Notes:

176 Name:
B: / / M: / / D: / /

177 Name:
B: / / M: / / D: / /

89 Name:
B: / / M: / / D: / /
Occupation:
Notes:

178 Name:
B: / / M: / / D: / /

179 Name:
B: / / M: / / D: / /

90 Name:
B: / / M: / / D: / /
Occupation:
Notes:

180 Name:
B: / / M: / / D: / /

181 Name:
B: / / M: / / D: / /

91 Name:
B: / / M: / / D: / /
Occupation:
Notes:

182 Name:
B: / / M: / / D: / /

183 Name:
B: / / M: / / D: / /

92 Name:
B: / / M: / / D: / /
Occupation:
Notes:

184 Name:
B: / / M: / / D: / /

185 Name:
B: / / M: / / D: / /

93 Name:
B: / / M: / / D: / /
Occupation:
Notes:

186 Name:
B: / / M: / / D: / /

187 Name:
B: / / M: / / D: / /

94 Name:
B: / / M: / / D: / /
Occupation:
Notes:

188 Name:
B: / / M: / / D: / /

189 Name:
B: / / M: / / D: / /

95 Name:
B: / / M: / / D: / /
Occupation:
Notes:

190 Name:
B: / / M: / / D: / /

191 Name:
B: / / M: / / D: / /

GENERATIONS 5 TO 8

(MATERNAL ANCESTORS)

GREAT-GREAT-GREAT-GRANDPARENTS

48 Name:
B: / / M: / / D: / /
Occupation:
Notes:

GREAT-GREAT-GRANDPARENTS

24 Name:
B: / / M: / / D: / /
Occupation:
Notes:

49 Name:
B: / / M: / / D: / /
Occupation:
Notes:

12

50 Name:
B: / / M: / / D: / /
Occupation:
Notes:

25 Name:
B: / / M: / / D: / /
Occupation:
Notes:

51 Name:
B: / / M: / / D: / /
Occupation:
Notes:

96 Name:
B: / / M: / / D: / /
Occupation:
Notes:

97 Name:
B: / / M: / / D: / /
Occupation:
Notes:

98 Name:
B: / / M: / / D: / /
Occupation:
Notes:

99 Name:
B: / / M: / / D: / /
Occupation:
Notes:

100 Name:
B: / / M: / / D: / /
Occupation:
Notes:

101 Name:
B: / / M: / / D: / /
Occupation:
Notes:

102 Name:
B: / / M: / / D: / /
Occupation:
Notes:

103 Name:
B: / / M: / / D: / /
Occupation:
Notes:

192 Name:
B: / / M: / / D: / /

193 Name:
B: / / M: / / D: / /

194 Name:
B: / / M: / / D: / /

195 Name:
B: / / M: / / D: / /

196 Name:
B: / / M: / / D: / /

197 Name:
B: / / M: / / D: / /

198 Name:
B: / / M: / / D: / /

199 Name:
B: / / M: / / D: / /

200 Name:
B: / / M: / / D: / /

201 Name:
B: / / M: / / D: / /

202 Name:
B: / / M: / / D: / /

203 Name:
B: / / M: / / D: / /

204 Name:
B: / / M: / / D: / /

205 Name:
B: / / M: / / D: / /

206 Name:
B: / / M: / / D: / /

207 Name:
B: / / M: / / D: / /

GENERATIONS 5 TO 8
(MATERNAL ANCESTORS)

GREAT-GREAT-GREAT-GRANDPARENTS

52 Name:
B: / / M: / / D: / /
Occupation:
Notes:

GREAT-GREAT-GRANDPARENTS

26 Name:
B: / / M: / / D: / /
Occupation:
Notes:

53 Name:
B: / / M: / / D: / /
Occupation:
Notes:

13

54 Name:
B: / / M: / / D: / /
Occupation:
Notes:

27 Name:
B: / / M: / / D: / /
Occupation:
Notes:

55 Name:
B: / / M: / / D: / /
Occupation:
Notes:

104 Name:
B: / / M: / / D: / /
Occupation:
Notes:

208 Name:
B: / / M: / / D: / /

209 Name:
B: / / M: / / D: / /

105 Name:
B: / / M: / / D: / /
Occupation:
Notes:

210 Name:
B: / / M: / / D: / /

211 Name:
B: / / M: / / D: / /

106 Name:
B: / / M: / / D: / /
Occupation:
Notes:

212 Name:
B: / / M: / / D: / /

213 Name:
B: / / M: / / D: / /

107 Name:
B: / / M: / / D: / /
Occupation:
Notes:

214 Name:
B: / / M: / / D: / /

215 Name:
B: / / M: / / D: / /

108 Name:
B: / / M: / / D: / /
Occupation:
Notes:

216 Name:
B: / / M: / / D: / /

217 Name:
B: / / M: / / D: / /

109 Name:
B: / / M: / / D: / /
Occupation:
Notes:

218 Name:
B: / / M: / / D: / /

219 Name:
B: / / M: / / D: / /

110 Name:
B: / / M: / / D: / /
Occupation:
Notes:

220 Name:
B: / / M: / / D: / /

221 Name:
B: / / M: / / D: / /

111 Name:
B: / / M: / / D: / /
Occupation:
Notes:

222 Name:
B: / / M: / / D: / /

223 Name:
B: / / M: / / D: / /

GENERATIONS 5 TO 8
(MATERNAL ANCESTORS)

GREAT-GREAT-GRANDPARENTS

28 Name:
B: / / M: / / D: / /
Occupation:
Notes:

14

29 Name:
B: / / M: / / D: / /
Occupation:
Notes:

GREAT-GREAT-GREAT-GRANDPARENTS

56 Name:
B: / / M: / / D: / /
Occupation:
Notes:

57 Name:
B: / / M: / / D: / /
Occupation:
Notes:

58 Name:
B: / / M: / / D: / /
Occupation:
Notes:

59 Name:
B: / / M: / / D: / /
Occupation:
Notes:

112 Name:
B: / / M: / / D: / /
Occupation:
Notes:

224 Name:
B: / / M: / / D: / /

225 Name:
B: / / M: / / D: / /

113 Name:
B: / / M: / / D: / /
Occupation:
Notes:

226 Name:
B: / / M: / / D: / /

227 Name:
B: / / M: / / D: / /

114 Name:
B: / / M: / / D: / /
Occupation:
Notes:

228 Name:
B: / / M: / / D: / /

229 Name:
B: / / M: / / D: / /

115 Name:
B: / / M: / / D: / /
Occupation:
Notes:

230 Name:
B: / / M: / / D: / /

231 Name:
B: / / M: / / D: / /

116 Name:
B: / / M: / / D: / /
Occupation:
Notes:

232 Name:
B: / / M: / / D: / /

233 Name:
B: / / M: / / D: / /

117 Name:
B: / / M: / / D: / /
Occupation:
Notes:

234 Name:
B: / / M: / / D: / /

235 Name:
B: / / M: / / D: / /

118 Name:
B: / / M: / / D: / /
Occupation:
Notes:

236 Name:
B: / / M: / / D: / /

237 Name:
B: / / M: / / D: / /

119 Name:
B: / / M: / / D: / /
Occupation:
Notes:

238 Name:
B: / / M: / / D: / /

239 Name:
B: / / M: / / D: / /

GENERATIONS 5 TO 8
(MATERNAL ANCESTORS)

GREAT-GREAT-GRANDPARENTS

30 Name:
B: / / M: / / D: / /
Occupation:
Notes:

15

31 Name:
B: / / M: / / D: / /
Occupation:
Notes:

GREAT-GREAT-GREAT-GRANDPARENTS

60 Name:
B: / / M: / / D: / /
Occupation:
Notes:

61 Name:
B: / / M: / / D: / /
Occupation:
Notes:

62 Name:
B: / / M: / / D: / /
Occupation:
Notes:

63 Name:
B: / / M: / / D: / /
Occupation:
Notes:

120 Name:
B: / / M: / / D: / /
Occupation:
Notes:

240 Name:
B: / / M: / / D: / /

241 Name:
B: / / M: / / D: / /

121 Name:
B: / / M: / / D: / /
Occupation:
Notes:

242 Name:
B: / / M: / / D: / /

243 Name:
B: / / M: / / D: / /

122 Name:
B: / / M: / / D: / /
Occupation:
Notes:

244 Name:
B: / / M: / / D: / /

245 Name:
B: / / M: / / D: / /

123 Name:
B: / / M: / / D: / /
Occupation:
Notes:

246 Name:
B: / / M: / / D: / /

247 Name:
B: / / M: / / D: / /

124 Name:
B: / / M: / / D: / /
Occupation:
Notes:

248 Name:
B: / / M: / / D: / /

249 Name:
B: / / M: / / D: / /

125 Name:
B: / / M: / / D: / /
Occupation:
Notes:

250 Name:
B: / / M: / / D: / /

251 Name:
B: / / M: / / D: / /

126 Name:
B: / / M: / / D: / /
Occupation:
Notes:

252 Name:
B: / / M: / / D: / /

253 Name:
B: / / M: / / D: / /

127 Name:
B: / / M: / / D: / /
Occupation:
Notes:

254 Name:
B: / / M: / / D: / /

255 Name:
B: / / M: / / D: / /

2 Name FATHER

DATE	SOURCE	INFORMATION
/ /		Birth
/ /		Baptism
/ /		
/ /		
/ /		
/ /		
/ /		
/ /		
/ /		
/ /		
/ /		
/ /		
/ /		
/ /		
/ /		Death
/ /		Burial

...the spouse of...

3 Name MOTHER

DATE	SOURCE	INFORMATION
/ /		Birth
/ /		Baptism
/ /		
/ /		
/ /		
/ /		
/ /		
/ /		
/ /		
/ /		
/ /		
/ /		
/ /		
/ /		
/ /		Death
/ /		Burial

Paternal Grandfather **Name 4**

DATE	SOURCE	INFORMATION
/ /		Birth
/ /		Baptism
/ /		
/ /		
/ /		
/ /		
/ /		
/ /		
/ /		
/ /		
/ /		
/ /		
/ /		
/ /		
/ /		Death
/ /		Burial

...the spouse of...

Paternal Grandmother **Name 5**

DATE	SOURCE	INFORMATION
/ /		Birth
/ /		Baptism
/ /		
/ /		
/ /		
/ /		
/ /		
/ /		
/ /		
/ /		
/ /		
/ /		
/ /		
/ /		
/ /		Death
/ /		Burial

6 Name MATERNAL GRANDFATHER

DATE	SOURCE	INFORMATION
/ /		Birth
/ /		Baptism
/ /		
/ /		
/ /		
/ /		
/ /		
/ /		
/ /		
/ /		
/ /		
/ /		
/ /		
/ /		
/ /		Death
/ /		Burial

...the spouse of...

7 Name MATERNAL GRANDMOTHER

DATE	SOURCE	INFORMATION
/ /		Birth
/ /		Baptism
/ /		
/ /		
/ /		
/ /		
/ /		
/ /		
/ /		
/ /		
/ /		
/ /		
/ /		
/ /		
/ /		Death
/ /		Burial

GREAT-GRANDFATHER (FATHER'S SIDE) **Name** **8**

DATE	SOURCE	INFORMATION
/ /		Birth
/ /		Baptism
/ /		
/ /		
/ /		
/ /		
/ /		
/ /		
/ /		
/ /		
/ /		
/ /		
/ /		
/ /		
/ /		Death
/ /		Burial

...the spouse of...

GREAT-GRANDMOTHER (FATHER'S SIDE) **Name** **9**

DATE	SOURCE	INFORMATION
/ /		Birth
/ /		Baptism
/ /		
/ /		
/ /		
/ /		
/ /		
/ /		
/ /		
/ /		
/ /		
/ /		
/ /		
/ /		
/ /		Death
/ /		Burial

10 Name GREAT-GRANDFATHER (FATHER'S SIDE)

DATE	SOURCE	INFORMATION
/ /		Birth
/ /		Baptism
/ /		
/ /		
/ /		
/ /		
/ /		
/ /		
/ /		
/ /		
/ /		
/ /		
/ /		
/ /		
/ /		Death
/ /		Burial

...the spouse of...

11 Name GREAT-GRANDMOTHER (FATHER'S SIDE)

DATE	SOURCE	INFORMATION
/ /		Birth
/ /		Baptism
/ /		
/ /		
/ /		
/ /		
/ /		
/ /		
/ /		
/ /		
/ /		
/ /		
/ /		
/ /		
/ /		Death
/ /		Burial

Great-Grandfather (mother's side) **Name** **12**

DATE	SOURCE	INFORMATION
/ /		Birth
/ /		Baptism
/ /		
/ /		
/ /		
/ /		
/ /		
/ /		
/ /		
/ /		
/ /		
/ /		
/ /		
/ /		
/ /		Death
/ /		Burial

...the spouse of...

Great-Grandmother (mother's side) **Name** **13**

DATE	SOURCE	INFORMATION
/ /		Birth
/ /		Baptism
/ /		
/ /		
/ /		
/ /		
/ /		
/ /		
/ /		
/ /		
/ /		
/ /		
/ /		
/ /		
/ /		Death
/ /		Burial

14 Name GREAT-GRANDFATHER (MOTHER'S SIDE)

DATE	SOURCE	INFORMATION
/ /		Birth
/ /		Baptism
/ /		
/ /		
/ /		
/ /		
/ /		
/ /		
/ /		
/ /		
/ /		
/ /		
/ /		
/ /		
/ /		Death
/ /		Burial

...the spouse of...

15 Name GREAT-GRANDMOTHER (MOTHER'S SIDE)

DATE	SOURCE	INFORMATION
/ /		Birth
/ /		Baptism
/ /		
/ /		
/ /		
/ /		
/ /		
/ /		
/ /		
/ /		
/ /		
/ /		
/ /		
/ /		
/ /		Death
/ /		Burial

2X-GRANDFATHER (FATHER'S SIDE) **Name** **16**

DATE	SOURCE	INFORMATION
/ /		Birth
/ /		Baptism
/ /		
/ /		
/ /		
/ /		
/ /		
/ /		
/ /		
/ /		
/ /		
/ /		
/ /		
/ /		
/ /		Death
/ /		Burial

...the spouse of...

2X-GRANDMOTHER (FATHER'S SIDE) **Name** **17**

DATE	SOURCE	INFORMATION
/ /		Birth
/ /		Baptism
/ /		
/ /		
/ /		
/ /		
/ /		
/ /		
/ /		
/ /		
/ /		
/ /		
/ /		
/ /		
/ /		Death
/ /		Burial

18 Name

2X-GRANDFATHER (FATHER'S SIDE)

DATE	SOURCE	INFORMATION
/ /		Birth
/ /		Baptism
/ /		
/ /		
/ /		
/ /		
/ /		
/ /		
/ /		
/ /		
/ /		
/ /		
/ /		
/ /		
/ /		Death
/ /		Burial

...the spouse of...

19 Name

2X-GRANDMOTHER (FATHER'S SIDE)

DATE	SOURCE	INFORMATION
/ /		Birth
/ /		Baptism
/ /		
/ /		
/ /		
/ /		
/ /		
/ /		
/ /		
/ /		
/ /		
/ /		
/ /		
/ /		
/ /		Death
/ /		Burial

2X-GRANDFATHER (FATHER'S SIDE) **Name** **20**

DATE	SOURCE	INFORMATION
/ /		Birth
/ /		Baptism
/ /		
/ /		
/ /		
/ /		
/ /		
/ /		
/ /		
/ /		
/ /		
/ /		
/ /		
/ /		
/ /		Death
/ /		Burial

...the spouse of...

2X-GRANDMOTHER (FATHER'S SIDE) **Name** **21**

DATE	SOURCE	INFORMATION
/ /		Birth
/ /		Baptism
/ /		
/ /		
/ /		
/ /		
/ /		
/ /		
/ /		
/ /		
/ /		
/ /		
/ /		
/ /		
/ /		Death
/ /		Burial

22 Name

2X-GRANDFATHER (FATHER'S SIDE)

DATE	SOURCE	INFORMATION
/ /		Birth
/ /		Baptism
/ /		
/ /		
/ /		
/ /		
/ /		
/ /		
/ /		
/ /		
/ /		
/ /		
/ /		
/ /		
/ /		Death
/ /		Burial

...the spouse of...

23 Name

2X-GRANDMOTHER (FATHER'S SIDE)

DATE	SOURCE	INFORMATION
/ /		Birth
/ /		Baptism
/ /		
/ /		
/ /		
/ /		
/ /		
/ /		
/ /		
/ /		
/ /		
/ /		
/ /		
/ /		
/ /		Death
/ /		Burial

2X-GRANDFATHER (MOTHER'S SIDE) **Name** **24**

DATE	SOURCE	INFORMATION
/ /		Birth
/ /		Baptism
/ /		
/ /		
/ /		
/ /		
/ /		
/ /		
/ /		
/ /		
/ /		
/ /		
/ /		
/ /		
/ /		Death
/ /		Burial

...the spouse of...

2X-GRANDMOTHER (MOTHER'S SIDE) **Name** **25**

DATE	SOURCE	INFORMATION
/ /		Birth
/ /		Baptism
/ /		
/ /		
/ /		
/ /		
/ /		
/ /		
/ /		
/ /		
/ /		
/ /		
/ /		
/ /		
/ /		Death
/ /		Burial

26 Name

2X-GRANDFATHER (MOTHER'S SIDE)

DATE	SOURCE	INFORMATION
/ /		Birth
/ /		Baptism
/ /		
/ /		
/ /		
/ /		
/ /		
/ /		
/ /		
/ /		
/ /		
/ /		
/ /		
/ /		
/ /		Death
/ /		Burial

...the spouse of...

27 Name

2X-GRANDMOTHER (MOTHER'S SIDE)

DATE	SOURCE	INFORMATION
/ /		Birth
/ /		Baptism
/ /		
/ /		
/ /		
/ /		
/ /		
/ /		
/ /		
/ /		
/ /		
/ /		
/ /		
/ /		
/ /		Death
/ /		Burial

2x-Grandfather (mother's side) **Name** **28**

DATE	SOURCE	INFORMATION
/ /		Birth
/ /		Baptism
/ /		
/ /		
/ /		
/ /		
/ /		
/ /		
/ /		
/ /		
/ /		
/ /		
/ /		
/ /		
/ /		Death
/ /		Burial

...the spouse of...

2x-Grandmother (mother's side) **Name** **29**

DATE	SOURCE	INFORMATION
/ /		Birth
/ /		Baptism
/ /		
/ /		
/ /		
/ /		
/ /		
/ /		
/ /		
/ /		
/ /		
/ /		
/ /		
/ /		
/ /		Death
/ /		Burial

30 Name 2X-GRANDFATHER (MOTHER'S SIDE)

DATE	SOURCE	INFORMATION
/ /		Birth
/ /		Baptism
/ /		
/ /		
/ /		
/ /		
/ /		
/ /		
/ /		
/ /		
/ /		
/ /		
/ /		
/ /		
/ /		Death
/ /		Burial

...the spouse of...

31 Name 2X-GRANDMOTHER (MOTHER'S SIDE)

DATE	SOURCE	INFORMATION
/ /		Birth
/ /		Baptism
/ /		
/ /		
/ /		
/ /		
/ /		
/ /		
/ /		
/ /		
/ /		
/ /		
/ /		
/ /		
/ /		Death
/ /		Burial

3X-GRANDFATHER (FATHER'S SIDE) **Name** **32**

DATE	SOURCE	INFORMATION
/ /		Birth
/ /		Baptism
/ /		
/ /		
/ /		
/ /		
/ /		
/ /		
/ /		
/ /		
/ /		
/ /		
/ /		
/ /		
/ /		Death
/ /		Burial

...the spouse of...

3X-GRANDMOTHER (FATHER'S SIDE) **Name** **33**

DATE	SOURCE	INFORMATION
/ /		Birth
/ /		Baptism
/ /		
/ /		
/ /		
/ /		
/ /		
/ /		
/ /		
/ /		
/ /		
/ /		
/ /		
/ /		
/ /		Death
/ /		Burial

34 Name

3x-Grandfather (father's side)

DATE	SOURCE	INFORMATION
/ /		Birth
/ /		Baptism
/ /		
/ /		
/ /		
/ /		
/ /		
/ /		
/ /		
/ /		
/ /		
/ /		
/ /		
/ /		
/ /		Death
/ /		Burial

...the spouse of...

35 Name

3x-Grandmother (father's side)

DATE	SOURCE	INFORMATION
/ /		Birth
/ /		Baptism
/ /		
/ /		
/ /		
/ /		
/ /		
/ /		
/ /		
/ /		
/ /		
/ /		
/ /		
/ /		
/ /		Death
/ /		Burial

3x-GRANDFATHER (FATHER'S SIDE) **Name** **36**

DATE	SOURCE	INFORMATION
/ /		Birth
/ /		Baptism
/ /		
/ /		
/ /		
/ /		
/ /		
/ /		
/ /		
/ /		
/ /		
/ /		
/ /		
/ /		
/ /		Death
/ /		Burial

...the spouse of...

3x-GRANDMOTHER (FATHER'S SIDE) **Name** **37**

DATE	SOURCE	INFORMATION
/ /		Birth
/ /		Baptism
/ /		
/ /		
/ /		
/ /		
/ /		
/ /		
/ /		
/ /		
/ /		
/ /		
/ /		
/ /		
/ /		Death
/ /		Burial

38 Name

3X-GRANDFATHER (FATHER'S SIDE)

DATE	SOURCE	INFORMATION
/ /		Birth
/ /		Baptism
/ /		
/ /		
/ /		
/ /		
/ /		
/ /		
/ /		
/ /		
/ /		
/ /		
/ /		
/ /		
/ /		Death
/ /		Burial

...the spouse of...

39 Name

3X-GRANDMOTHER (FATHER'S SIDE)

DATE	SOURCE	INFORMATION
/ /		Birth
/ /		Baptism
/ /		
/ /		
/ /		
/ /		
/ /		
/ /		
/ /		
/ /		
/ /		
/ /		
/ /		
/ /		
/ /		Death
/ /		Burial

3X-GRANDFATHER (FATHER'S SIDE) **Name** **40**

DATE	SOURCE	INFORMATION
/ /		Birth
/ /		Baptism
/ /		
/ /		
/ /		
/ /		
/ /		
/ /		
/ /		
/ /		
/ /		
/ /		
/ /		
/ /		
/ /		Death
/ /		Burial

...the spouse of...

3X-GRANDMOTHER (FATHER'S SIDE) **Name** **41**

DATE	SOURCE	INFORMATION
/ /		Birth
/ /		Baptism
/ /		
/ /		
/ /		
/ /		
/ /		
/ /		
/ /		
/ /		
/ /		
/ /		
/ /		
/ /		
/ /		Death
/ /		Burial

42 Name 3X-GRANDFATHER (FATHER'S SIDE)

DATE	SOURCE	INFORMATION
/ /		Birth
/ /		Baptism
/ /		
/ /		
/ /		
/ /		
/ /		
/ /		
/ /		
/ /		
/ /		
/ /		
/ /		
/ /		
/ /		Death
/ /		Burial

...the spouse of...

43 Name 3X-GRANDMOTHER (FATHER'S SIDE)

DATE	SOURCE	INFORMATION
/ /		Birth
/ /		Baptism
/ /		
/ /		
/ /		
/ /		
/ /		
/ /		
/ /		
/ /		
/ /		
/ /		
/ /		
/ /		
/ /		Death
/ /		Burial

3X-GRANDFATHER (FATHER'S SIDE) **Name** **44**

DATE	SOURCE	INFORMATION
/ /		Birth
/ /		Baptism
/ /		
/ /		
/ /		
/ /		
/ /		
/ /		
/ /		
/ /		
/ /		
/ /		
/ /		
/ /		
/ /		Death
/ /		Burial

...the spouse of...

3X-GRANDMOTHER (FATHER'S SIDE) **Name** **45**

DATE	SOURCE	INFORMATION
/ /		Birth
/ /		Baptism
/ /		
/ /		
/ /		
/ /		
/ /		
/ /		
/ /		
/ /		
/ /		
/ /		
/ /		
/ /		
/ /		Death
/ /		Burial

46 Name 3x-GRANDFATHER (FATHER'S SIDE)

DATE	SOURCE	INFORMATION
/ /		Birth
/ /		Baptism
/ /		
/ /		
/ /		
/ /		
/ /		
/ /		
/ /		
/ /		
/ /		
/ /		
/ /		
/ /		
/ /		Death
/ /		Burial

...the spouse of...

47 Name 3x-GRANDMOTHER (FATHER'S SIDE)

DATE	SOURCE	INFORMATION
/ /		Birth
/ /		Baptism
/ /		
/ /		
/ /		
/ /		
/ /		
/ /		
/ /		
/ /		
/ /		
/ /		
/ /		
/ /		
/ /		Death
/ /		Burial

3x-GRANDFATHER (MOTHER'S SIDE) **Name** **48**

DATE	SOURCE	INFORMATION
/ /		Birth
/ /		Baptism
/ /		
/ /		
/ /		
/ /		
/ /		
/ /		
/ /		
/ /		
/ /		
/ /		
/ /		
/ /		
/ /		Death
/ /		Burial

...the spouse of...

3x-GRANDMOTHER (MOTHER'S SIDE) **Name** **49**

DATE	SOURCE	INFORMATION
/ /		Birth
/ /		Baptism
/ /		
/ /		
/ /		
/ /		
/ /		
/ /		
/ /		
/ /		
/ /		
/ /		
/ /		
/ /		
/ /		Death
/ /		Burial

50 Name 3x-Grandfather (mother's side)

DATE	SOURCE	INFORMATION
/ /		Birth
/ /		Baptism
/ /		
/ /		
/ /		
/ /		
/ /		
/ /		
/ /		
/ /		
/ /		
/ /		
/ /		
/ /		
/ /		Death
/ /		Burial

...the spouse of...

51 Name 3x-Grandmother (mother's side)

DATE	SOURCE	INFORMATION
/ /		Birth
/ /		Baptism
/ /		
/ /		
/ /		
/ /		
/ /		
/ /		
/ /		
/ /		
/ /		
/ /		
/ /		
/ /		
/ /		Death
/ /		Burial

3x-Grandfather (mother's side) **Name** **52**

DATE	SOURCE	INFORMATION
/ /		Birth
/ /		Baptism
/ /		
/ /		
/ /		
/ /		
/ /		
/ /		
/ /		
/ /		
/ /		
/ /		
/ /		
/ /		
/ /		Death
/ /		Burial

...the spouse of...

3x-Grandmother (mother's side) **Name** **53**

DATE	SOURCE	INFORMATION
/ /		Birth
/ /		Baptism
/ /		
/ /		
/ /		
/ /		
/ /		
/ /		
/ /		
/ /		
/ /		
/ /		
/ /		
/ /		
/ /		Death
/ /		Burial

54 Name 3X-GRANDFATHER (MOTHER'S SIDE)

DATE	SOURCE	INFORMATION
/ /		Birth
/ /		Baptism
/ /		
/ /		
/ /		
/ /		
/ /		
/ /		
/ /		
/ /		
/ /		
/ /		
/ /		
/ /		
/ /		Death
/ /		Burial

...the spouse of...

55 Name 3X-GRANDMOTHER (MOTHER'S SIDE)

DATE	SOURCE	INFORMATION
/ /		Birth
/ /		Baptism
/ /		
/ /		
/ /		
/ /		
/ /		
/ /		
/ /		
/ /		
/ /		
/ /		
/ /		
/ /		
/ /		Death
/ /		Burial

3x-GRANDFATHER (MOTHER'S SIDE) **Name** **56**

DATE	SOURCE	INFORMATION
/ /		Birth
/ /		Baptism
/ /		
/ /		
/ /		
/ /		
/ /		
/ /		
/ /		
/ /		
/ /		
/ /		
/ /		
/ /		
/ /		Death
/ /		Burial

...the spouse of...

3x-GRANDMOTHER (MOTHER'S SIDE) **Name** **57**

DATE	SOURCE	INFORMATION
/ /		Birth
/ /		Baptism
/ /		
/ /		
/ /		
/ /		
/ /		
/ /		
/ /		
/ /		
/ /		
/ /		
/ /		
/ /		
/ /		Death
/ /		Burial

58 Name

3X-GRANDFATHER (MOTHER'S SIDE)

DATE	SOURCE	INFORMATION
/ /		Birth
/ /		Baptism
/ /		
/ /		
/ /		
/ /		
/ /		
/ /		
/ /		
/ /		
/ /		
/ /		
/ /		
/ /		
/ /		Death
/ /		Burial

...the spouse of...

59 Name

3X-GRANDMOTHER (MOTHER'S SIDE)

DATE	SOURCE	INFORMATION
/ /		Birth
/ /		Baptism
/ /		
/ /		
/ /		
/ /		
/ /		
/ /		
/ /		
/ /		
/ /		
/ /		
/ /		
/ /		
/ /		Death
/ /		Burial

3x-Grandfather (mother's side) **Name** **60**

DATE	SOURCE	INFORMATION
/ /		Birth
/ /		Baptism
/ /		
/ /		
/ /		
/ /		
/ /		
/ /		
/ /		
/ /		
/ /		
/ /		
/ /		
/ /		
/ /		Death
/ /		Burial

...the spouse of...

3x-Grandmother (mother's side) **Name** **61**

DATE	SOURCE	INFORMATION
/ /		Birth
/ /		Baptism
/ /		
/ /		
/ /		
/ /		
/ /		
/ /		
/ /		
/ /		
/ /		
/ /		
/ /		
/ /		
/ /		Death
/ /		Burial

62 Name 3X-GRANDFATHER (MOTHER'S SIDE)

DATE	SOURCE	INFORMATION
/ /		Birth
/ /		Baptism
/ /		
/ /		
/ /		
/ /		
/ /		
/ /		
/ /		
/ /		
/ /		
/ /		
/ /		
/ /		
/ /		Death
/ /		Burial

...the spouse of...

63 Name 3X-GRANDMOTHER (MOTHER'S SIDE)

DATE	SOURCE	INFORMATION
/ /		Birth
/ /		Baptism
/ /		
/ /		
/ /		
/ /		
/ /		
/ /		
/ /		
/ /		
/ /		
/ /		
/ /		
/ /		
/ /		Death
/ /		Burial

4X-GRANDFATHER (FATHER'S SIDE) **Name** **64**

DATE	SOURCE	INFORMATION
/ /		Birth
/ /		Baptism
/ /		
/ /		
/ /		
/ /		
/ /		
/ /		
/ /		
/ /		
/ /		
/ /		
/ /		
/ /		
/ /		Death
/ /		Burial

...the spouse of...

4X-GRANDMOTHER (FATHER'S SIDE) **Name** **65**

DATE	SOURCE	INFORMATION
/ /		Birth
/ /		Baptism
/ /		
/ /		
/ /		
/ /		
/ /		
/ /		
/ /		
/ /		
/ /		
/ /		
/ /		
/ /		
/ /		Death
/ /		Burial

66 Name

4X-GRANDFATHER (FATHER'S SIDE)

DATE	SOURCE	INFORMATION
/ /		Birth
/ /		Baptism
/ /		
/ /		
/ /		
/ /		
/ /		
/ /		
/ /		
/ /		
/ /		
/ /		
/ /		
/ /		
/ /		Death
/ /		Burial

...the spouse of...

67 Name

4X-GRANDMOTHER (FATHER'S SIDE)

DATE	SOURCE	INFORMATION
/ /		Birth
/ /		Baptism
/ /		
/ /		
/ /		
/ /		
/ /		
/ /		
/ /		
/ /		
/ /		
/ /		
/ /		
/ /		
/ /		Death
/ /		Burial

4X-GRANDFATHER (FATHER'S SIDE) **Name** **68**

DATE	SOURCE	INFORMATION
/ /		Birth
/ /		Baptism
/ /		
/ /		
/ /		
/ /		
/ /		
/ /		
/ /		
/ /		
/ /		
/ /		
/ /		
/ /		
/ /		Death
/ /		Burial

...the spouse of...

4X-GRANDMOTHER (FATHER'S SIDE) **Name** **69**

DATE	SOURCE	INFORMATION
/ /		Birth
/ /		Baptism
/ /		
/ /		
/ /		
/ /		
/ /		
/ /		
/ /		
/ /		
/ /		
/ /		
/ /		
/ /		
/ /		Death
/ /		Burial

70 Name

4X-GRANDFATHER (FATHER'S SIDE)

DATE	SOURCE	INFORMATION
/ /		Birth
/ /		Baptism
/ /		
/ /		
/ /		
/ /		
/ /		
/ /		
/ /		
/ /		
/ /		
/ /		
/ /		
/ /		
/ /		Death
/ /		Burial

...the spouse of...

71 Name

4X-GRANDMOTHER (FATHER'S SIDE)

DATE	SOURCE	INFORMATION
/ /		Birth
/ /		Baptism
/ /		
/ /		
/ /		
/ /		
/ /		
/ /		
/ /		
/ /		
/ /		
/ /		
/ /		
/ /		
/ /		Death
/ /		Burial

4X-GRANDFATHER (FATHER'S SIDE) **Name** **72**

DATE	SOURCE	INFORMATION
/ /		Birth
/ /		Baptism
/ /		
/ /		
/ /		
/ /		
/ /		
/ /		
/ /		
/ /		
/ /		
/ /		
/ /		
/ /		
/ /		Death
/ /		Burial

...the spouse of...

4X-GRANDMOTHER (FATHER'S SIDE) **Name** **73**

DATE	SOURCE	INFORMATION
/ /		Birth
/ /		Baptism
/ /		
/ /		
/ /		
/ /		
/ /		
/ /		
/ /		
/ /		
/ /		
/ /		
/ /		
/ /		
/ /		Death
/ /		Burial

74 Name 4X-GRANDFATHER (FATHER'S SIDE)

DATE	SOURCE	INFORMATION
/ /		Birth
/ /		Baptism
/ /		
/ /		
/ /		
/ /		
/ /		
/ /		
/ /		
/ /		
/ /		
/ /		
/ /		
/ /		
/ /		Death
/ /		Burial

...the spouse of...

75 Name 4X-GRANDMOTHER (FATHER'S SIDE)

DATE	SOURCE	INFORMATION
/ /		Birth
/ /		Baptism
/ /		
/ /		
/ /		
/ /		
/ /		
/ /		
/ /		
/ /		
/ /		
/ /		
/ /		
/ /		
/ /		Death
/ /		Burial

4X-GRANDFATHER (FATHER'S SIDE) **Name** **76**

DATE	SOURCE	INFORMATION
/ /		Birth
/ /		Baptism
/ /		
/ /		
/ /		
/ /		
/ /		
/ /		
/ /		
/ /		
/ /		
/ /		
/ /		
/ /		
/ /		Death
/ /		Burial

...the spouse of...

4X-GRANDMOTHER (FATHER'S SIDE) **Name** **77**

DATE	SOURCE	INFORMATION
/ /		Birth
/ /		Baptism
/ /		
/ /		
/ /		
/ /		
/ /		
/ /		
/ /		
/ /		
/ /		
/ /		
/ /		
/ /		
/ /		Death
/ /		Burial

78 Name 4x-GRANDFATHER (FATHER'S SIDE)

DATE	SOURCE	INFORMATION
/ /		Birth
/ /		Baptism
/ /		
/ /		
/ /		
/ /		
/ /		
/ /		
/ /		
/ /		
/ /		
/ /		
/ /		
/ /		
/ /		Death
/ /		Burial

...the spouse of...

79 Name 4x-GRANDMOTHER (FATHER'S SIDE)

DATE	SOURCE	INFORMATION
/ /		Birth
/ /		Baptism
/ /		
/ /		
/ /		
/ /		
/ /		
/ /		
/ /		
/ /		
/ /		
/ /		
/ /		
/ /		
/ /		Death
/ /		Burial

4X-GRANDFATHER (FATHER'S SIDE) **Name** **80**

DATE	SOURCE	INFORMATION
/ /		Birth
/ /		Baptism
/ /		
/ /		
/ /		
/ /		
/ /		
/ /		
/ /		
/ /		
/ /		
/ /		
/ /		
/ /		
/ /		Death
/ /		Burial

...the spouse of...

4X-GRANDMOTHER (FATHER'S SIDE) **Name** **81**

DATE	SOURCE	INFORMATION
/ /		Birth
/ /		Baptism
/ /		
/ /		
/ /		
/ /		
/ /		
/ /		
/ /		
/ /		
/ /		
/ /		
/ /		
/ /		
/ /		Death
/ /		Burial

82 Name

4X-GRANDFATHER (FATHER'S SIDE)

DATE	SOURCE	INFORMATION
/ /		Birth
/ /		Baptism
/ /		
/ /		
/ /		
/ /		
/ /		
/ /		
/ /		
/ /		
/ /		
/ /		
/ /		
/ /		
/ /		Death
/ /		Burial

...the spouse of...

83 Name

4X-GRANDMOTHER (FATHER'S SIDE)

DATE	SOURCE	INFORMATION
/ /		Birth
/ /		Baptism
/ /		
/ /		
/ /		
/ /		
/ /		
/ /		
/ /		
/ /		
/ /		
/ /		
/ /		
/ /		
/ /		Death
/ /		Burial

4x-Grandfather (father's side) **Name** **84**

DATE	SOURCE	INFORMATION
/ /		Birth
/ /		Baptism
/ /		
/ /		
/ /		
/ /		
/ /		
/ /		
/ /		
/ /		
/ /		
/ /		
/ /		
/ /		
/ /		Death
/ /		Burial

...the spouse of...

4x-Grandmother (father's side) **Name** **85**

DATE	SOURCE	INFORMATION
/ /		Birth
/ /		Baptism
/ /		
/ /		
/ /		
/ /		
/ /		
/ /		
/ /		
/ /		
/ /		
/ /		
/ /		
/ /		
/ /		Death
/ /		Burial

86 Name 4X-GRANDFATHER (FATHER'S SIDE)

DATE	SOURCE	INFORMATION
/ /		Birth
/ /		Baptism
/ /		
/ /		
/ /		
/ /		
/ /		
/ /		
/ /		
/ /		
/ /		
/ /		
/ /		
/ /		
/ /		Death
/ /		Burial

...the spouse of...

87 Name 4X-GRANDMOTHER (FATHER'S SIDE)

DATE	SOURCE	INFORMATION
/ /		Birth
/ /		Baptism
/ /		
/ /		
/ /		
/ /		
/ /		
/ /		
/ /		
/ /		
/ /		
/ /		
/ /		
/ /		
/ /		Death
/ /		Burial

4x-GRANDFATHER (FATHER'S SIDE) **Name** **88**

DATE	SOURCE	INFORMATION
/ /		Birth
/ /		Baptism
/ /		
/ /		
/ /		
/ /		
/ /		
/ /		
/ /		
/ /		
/ /		
/ /		
/ /		
/ /		
/ /		Death
/ /		Burial

...the spouse of...

4x-GRANDMOTHER (FATHER'S SIDE) **Name** **89**

DATE	SOURCE	INFORMATION
/ /		Birth
/ /		Baptism
/ /		
/ /		
/ /		
/ /		
/ /		
/ /		
/ /		
/ /		
/ /		
/ /		
/ /		
/ /		
/ /		Death
/ /		Burial

90 Name

4X-GRANDFATHER (FATHER'S SIDE)

DATE	SOURCE	INFORMATION
/ /		Birth
/ /		Baptism
/ /		
/ /		
/ /		
/ /		
/ /		
/ /		
/ /		
/ /		
/ /		
/ /		
/ /		
/ /		
/ /		Death
/ /		Burial

...the spouse of...

91 Name

4X-GRANDMOTHER (FATHER'S SIDE)

DATE	SOURCE	INFORMATION
/ /		Birth
/ /		Baptism
/ /		
/ /		
/ /		
/ /		
/ /		
/ /		
/ /		
/ /		
/ /		
/ /		
/ /		
/ /		
/ /		Death
/ /		Burial

4x-Grandfather (father's side) **Name** **92**

DATE	SOURCE	INFORMATION
/ /		Birth
/ /		Baptism
/ /		
/ /		
/ /		
/ /		
/ /		
/ /		
/ /		
/ /		
/ /		
/ /		
/ /		
/ /		
/ /		Death
/ /		Burial

...the spouse of...

4x-Grandmother (father's side) **Name** **93**

DATE	SOURCE	INFORMATION
/ /		Birth
/ /		Baptism
/ /		
/ /		
/ /		
/ /		
/ /		
/ /		
/ /		
/ /		
/ /		
/ /		
/ /		
/ /		
/ /		Death
/ /		Burial

94 **Name** 4x-Grandfather (father's side)

DATE	SOURCE	INFORMATION
/ /		Birth
/ /		Baptism
/ /		
/ /		
/ /		
/ /		
/ /		
/ /		
/ /		
/ /		
/ /		
/ /		
/ /		
/ /		
/ /		Death
/ /		Burial

...the spouse of...

95 **Name** 4x-Grandmother (father's side)

DATE	SOURCE	INFORMATION
/ /		Birth
/ /		Baptism
/ /		
/ /		
/ /		
/ /		
/ /		
/ /		
/ /		
/ /		
/ /		
/ /		
/ /		
/ /		
/ /		Death
/ /		Burial

4X-GRANDFATHER (MOTHER'S SIDE) **Name** **96**

DATE	SOURCE	INFORMATION
/ /		Birth
/ /		Baptism
/ /		
/ /		
/ /		
/ /		
/ /		
/ /		
/ /		
/ /		
/ /		
/ /		
/ /		
/ /		
/ /		Death
/ /		Burial

...the spouse of...

4X-GRANDMOTHER (MOTHER'S SIDE) **Name** **97**

DATE	SOURCE	INFORMATION
/ /		Birth
/ /		Baptism
/ /		
/ /		
/ /		
/ /		
/ /		
/ /		
/ /		
/ /		
/ /		
/ /		
/ /		
/ /		
/ /		Death
/ /		Burial

98 Name

4X-GRANDFATHER (MOTHER'S SIDE)

DATE	SOURCE	INFORMATION
/ /		Birth
/ /		Baptism
/ /		
/ /		
/ /		
/ /		
/ /		
/ /		
/ /		
/ /		
/ /		
/ /		
/ /		
/ /		
/ /		Death
/ /		Burial

...the spouse of...

99 Name

4X-GRANDMOTHER (MOTHER'S SIDE)

DATE	SOURCE	INFORMATION
/ /		Birth
/ /		Baptism
/ /		
/ /		
/ /		
/ /		
/ /		
/ /		
/ /		
/ /		
/ /		
/ /		
/ /		
/ /		
/ /		Death
/ /		Burial

4X-GRANDFATHER (MOTHER'S SIDE) **Name** **100**

DATE	SOURCE	INFORMATION
/ /		Birth
/ /		Baptism
/ /		
/ /		
/ /		
/ /		
/ /		
/ /		
/ /		
/ /		
/ /		
/ /		
/ /		
/ /		
/ /		Death
/ /		Burial

...the spouse of...

4X-GRANDMOTHER (MOTHER'S SIDE) **Name** **101**

DATE	SOURCE	INFORMATION
/ /		Birth
/ /		Baptism
/ /		
/ /		
/ /		
/ /		
/ /		
/ /		
/ /		
/ /		
/ /		
/ /		
/ /		
/ /		
/ /		Death
/ /		Burial

102 Name 4X-GRANDFATHER (MOTHER'S SIDE)

DATE	SOURCE	INFORMATION
/ /		Birth
/ /		Baptism
/ /		
/ /		
/ /		
/ /		
/ /		
/ /		
/ /		
/ /		
/ /		
/ /		
/ /		
/ /		
/ /		Death
/ /		Burial

...the spouse of...

103 Name 4X-GRANDMOTHER (MOTHER'S SIDE)

DATE	SOURCE	INFORMATION
/ /		Birth
/ /		Baptism
/ /		
/ /		
/ /		
/ /		
/ /		
/ /		
/ /		
/ /		
/ /		
/ /		
/ /		
/ /		
/ /		Death
/ /		Burial

4X-GRANDFATHER (MOTHER'S SIDE) **Name**

DATE	SOURCE	INFORMATION
/ /		Birth
/ /		Baptism
/ /		
/ /		
/ /		
/ /		
/ /		
/ /		
/ /		
/ /		
/ /		
/ /		
/ /		
/ /		
/ /		Death
/ /		Burial

...the spouse of...

4X-GRANDMOTHER (MOTHER'S SIDE) **Name** **105**

DATE	SOURCE	INFORMATION
/ /		Birth
/ /		Baptism
/ /		
/ /		
/ /		
/ /		
/ /		
/ /		
/ /		
/ /		
/ /		
/ /		
/ /		
/ /		
/ /		Death
/ /		Burial

106 Name 4x-Grandfather (mother's side)

DATE	SOURCE	INFORMATION
/ /		Birth
/ /		Baptism
/ /		
/ /		
/ /		
/ /		
/ /		
/ /		
/ /		
/ /		
/ /		
/ /		
/ /		
/ /		
/ /		Death
/ /		Burial

...the spouse of...

107 Name 4x-Grandmother (mother's side)

DATE	SOURCE	INFORMATION
/ /		Birth
/ /		Baptism
/ /		
/ /		
/ /		
/ /		
/ /		
/ /		
/ /		
/ /		
/ /		
/ /		
/ /		
/ /		
/ /		Death
/ /		Burial

4X-GRANDFATHER (MOTHER'S SIDE) **Name** **108**

DATE	SOURCE	INFORMATION
/ /		Birth
/ /		Baptism
/ /		
/ /		
/ /		
/ /		
/ /		
/ /		
/ /		
/ /		
/ /		
/ /		
/ /		
/ /		
/ /		Death
/ /		Burial

...the spouse of...

4X-GRANDMOTHER (MOTHER'S SIDE) **Name** **109**

DATE	SOURCE	INFORMATION
/ /		Birth
/ /		Baptism
/ /		
/ /		
/ /		
/ /		
/ /		
/ /		
/ /		
/ /		
/ /		
/ /		
/ /		
/ /		
/ /		Death
/ /		Burial

110 Name 4x-GRANDFATHER (MOTHER'S SIDE)

DATE	SOURCE	INFORMATION
/ /		Birth
/ /		Baptism
/ /		
/ /		
/ /		
/ /		
/ /		
/ /		
/ /		
/ /		
/ /		
/ /		
/ /		
/ /		
/ /		Death
/ /		Burial

...the spouse of...

111 Name 4x-GRANDMOTHER (MOTHER'S SIDE)

DATE	SOURCE	INFORMATION
/ /		Birth
/ /		Baptism
/ /		
/ /		
/ /		
/ /		
/ /		
/ /		
/ /		
/ /		
/ /		
/ /		
/ /		
/ /		
/ /		Death
/ /		Burial

4x-Grandfather (mother's side) **Name** **112**

DATE	SOURCE	INFORMATION
/ /		Birth
/ /		Baptism
/ /		
/ /		
/ /		
/ /		
/ /		
/ /		
/ /		
/ /		
/ /		
/ /		
/ /		
/ /		
/ /		Death
/ /		Burial

...the spouse of...

4x-Grandmother (mother's side) **Name** **113**

DATE	SOURCE	INFORMATION
/ /		Birth
/ /		Baptism
/ /		
/ /		
/ /		
/ /		
/ /		
/ /		
/ /		
/ /		
/ /		
/ /		
/ /		
/ /		
/ /		Death
/ /		Burial

114 Name

4X-GRANDFATHER (MOTHER'S SIDE)

DATE	SOURCE	INFORMATION
/ /		Birth
/ /		Baptism
/ /		
/ /		
/ /		
/ /		
/ /		
/ /		
/ /		
/ /		
/ /		
/ /		
/ /		
/ /		
/ /		Death
/ /		Burial

...the spouse of...

115 Name

4X-GRANDMOTHER (MOTHER'S SIDE)

DATE	SOURCE	INFORMATION
/ /		Birth
/ /		Baptism
/ /		
/ /		
/ /		
/ /		
/ /		
/ /		
/ /		
/ /		
/ /		
/ /		
/ /		
/ /		
/ /		Death
/ /		Burial

4x-Grandfather (mother's side) **Name** **116**

DATE	SOURCE	INFORMATION
/ /		Birth
/ /		Baptism
/ /		
/ /		
/ /		
/ /		
/ /		
/ /		
/ /		
/ /		
/ /		
/ /		
/ /		
/ /		
/ /		Death
/ /		Burial

...the spouse of...

4x-Grandmother (mother's side) **Name** **117**

DATE	SOURCE	INFORMATION
/ /		Birth
/ /		Baptism
/ /		
/ /		
/ /		
/ /		
/ /		
/ /		
/ /		
/ /		
/ /		
/ /		
/ /		
/ /		
/ /		Death
/ /		Burial

118 Name

4x-GRANDFATHER (MOTHER'S SIDE)

DATE	SOURCE	INFORMATION
/ /		Birth
/ /		Baptism
/ /		
/ /		
/ /		
/ /		
/ /		
/ /		
/ /		
/ /		
/ /		
/ /		
/ /		
/ /		
/ /		Death
/ /		Burial

...the spouse of...

119 Name

4x-GRANDMOTHER (MOTHER'S SIDE)

DATE	SOURCE	INFORMATION
/ /		Birth
/ /		Baptism
/ /		
/ /		
/ /		
/ /		
/ /		
/ /		
/ /		
/ /		
/ /		
/ /		
/ /		
/ /		
/ /		Death
/ /		Burial

4X-GRANDFATHER (MOTHER'S SIDE) **Name** **120**

DATE	SOURCE	INFORMATION
/ /		Birth
/ /		Baptism
/ /		
/ /		
/ /		
/ /		
/ /		
/ /		
/ /		
/ /		
/ /		
/ /		
/ /		
/ /		
/ /		Death
/ /		Burial

...the spouse of...

4X-GRANDMOTHER (MOTHER'S SIDE) **Name** **121**

DATE	SOURCE	INFORMATION
/ /		Birth
/ /		Baptism
/ /		
/ /		
/ /		
/ /		
/ /		
/ /		
/ /		
/ /		
/ /		
/ /		
/ /		
/ /		
/ /		Death
/ /		Burial

122 Name 4x-GRANDFATHER (MOTHER'S SIDE)

DATE	SOURCE	INFORMATION
/ /		Birth
/ /		Baptism
/ /		
/ /		
/ /		
/ /		
/ /		
/ /		
/ /		
/ /		
/ /		
/ /		
/ /		
/ /		
/ /		Death
/ /		Burial

...the spouse of...

123 Name 4x-GRANDMOTHER (MOTHER'S SIDE)

DATE	SOURCE	INFORMATION
/ /		Birth
/ /		Baptism
/ /		
/ /		
/ /		
/ /		
/ /		
/ /		
/ /		
/ /		
/ /		
/ /		
/ /		
/ /		
/ /		Death
/ /		Burial

4X-GRANDFATHER (MOTHER'S SIDE) **Name** **124**

DATE	SOURCE	INFORMATION
/ /		Birth
/ /		Baptism
/ /		
/ /		
/ /		
/ /		
/ /		
/ /		
/ /		
/ /		
/ /		
/ /		
/ /		
/ /		
/ /		Death
/ /		Burial

...the spouse of...

4X-GRANDMOTHER (MOTHER'S SIDE) **Name** **125**

DATE	SOURCE	INFORMATION
/ /		Birth
/ /		Baptism
/ /		
/ /		
/ /		
/ /		
/ /		
/ /		
/ /		
/ /		
/ /		
/ /		
/ /		
/ /		
/ /		Death
/ /		Burial

126 Name 4X-GRANDFATHER (MOTHER'S SIDE)

DATE	SOURCE	INFORMATION
/ /		Birth
/ /		Baptism
/ /		
/ /		
/ /		
/ /		
/ /		
/ /		
/ /		
/ /		
/ /		
/ /		
/ /		
/ /		
/ /		Death
/ /		Burial

...the spouse of...

127 Name 4X-GRANDMOTHER (MOTHER'S SIDE)

DATE	SOURCE	INFORMATION
/ /		Birth
/ /		Baptism
/ /		
/ /		
/ /		
/ /		
/ /		
/ /		
/ /		
/ /		
/ /		
/ /		
/ /		
/ /		
/ /		Death
/ /		Burial

5X-GRANDFATHER (FATHER'S SIDE) **Name** **128**

DATE	SOURCE	INFORMATION
/ /		Birth
/ /		Baptism
/ /		
/ /		
/ /		
/ /		
/ /		
/ /		
/ /		
/ /		
/ /		
/ /		
/ /		
/ /		
/ /		Death
/ /		Burial

...the spouse of...

5X-GRANDMOTHER (FATHER'S SIDE) **Name** **129**

DATE	SOURCE	INFORMATION
/ /		Birth
/ /		Baptism
/ /		
/ /		
/ /		
/ /		
/ /		
/ /		
/ /		
/ /		
/ /		
/ /		
/ /		
/ /		
/ /		Death
/ /		Burial

130 Name 5X-GRANDFATHER (FATHER'S SIDE)

DATE	SOURCE	INFORMATION
/ /		Birth
/ /		Baptism
/ /		
/ /		
/ /		
/ /		
/ /		
/ /		
/ /		
/ /		
/ /		
/ /		
/ /		
/ /		
/ /		Death
/ /		Burial

...the spouse of...

131 Name 5X-GRANDMOTHER (FATHER'S SIDE)

DATE	SOURCE	INFORMATION
/ /		Birth
/ /		Baptism
/ /		
/ /		
/ /		
/ /		
/ /		
/ /		
/ /		
/ /		
/ /		
/ /		
/ /		
/ /		
/ /		Death
/ /		Burial

5x-Grandfather (father's side) **Name** **132**

DATE	SOURCE	INFORMATION
/ /		Birth
/ /		Baptism
/ /		
/ /		
/ /		
/ /		
/ /		
/ /		
/ /		
/ /		
/ /		
/ /		
/ /		
/ /		
/ /		Death
/ /		Burial

...the spouse of...

5x-Grandmother (father's side) **Name** **133**

DATE	SOURCE	INFORMATION
/ /		Birth
/ /		Baptism
/ /		
/ /		
/ /		
/ /		
/ /		
/ /		
/ /		
/ /		
/ /		
/ /		
/ /		
/ /		
/ /		Death
/ /		Burial

134 **Name** 5x-GRANDFATHER (FATHER'S SIDE)

DATE	SOURCE	INFORMATION
/ /		Birth
/ /		Baptism
/ /		
/ /		
/ /		
/ /		
/ /		
/ /		
/ /		
/ /		
/ /		
/ /		
/ /		
/ /		
/ /		Death
/ /		Burial

...the spouse of...

135 **Name** 5x-GRANDMOTHER (FATHER'S SIDE)

DATE	SOURCE	INFORMATION
/ /		Birth
/ /		Baptism
/ /		
/ /		
/ /		
/ /		
/ /		
/ /		
/ /		
/ /		
/ /		
/ /		
/ /		
/ /		
/ /		Death
/ /		Burial

5X-GRANDFATHER (FATHER'S SIDE) **Name** **136**

DATE	SOURCE	INFORMATION
/ /		Birth
/ /		Baptism
/ /		
/ /		
/ /		
/ /		
/ /		
/ /		
/ /		
/ /		
/ /		
/ /		
/ /		
/ /		
/ /		Death
/ /		Burial

...the spouse of...

5X-GRANDMOTHER (FATHER'S SIDE) **Name** **137**

DATE	SOURCE	INFORMATION
/ /		Birth
/ /		Baptism
/ /		
/ /		
/ /		
/ /		
/ /		
/ /		
/ /		
/ /		
/ /		
/ /		
/ /		
/ /		
/ /		Death
/ /		Burial

138 Name 5X-GRANDFATHER (FATHER'S SIDE)

DATE	SOURCE	INFORMATION
/ /		Birth
/ /		Baptism
/ /		
/ /		
/ /		
/ /		
/ /		
/ /		
/ /		
/ /		
/ /		
/ /		
/ /		
/ /		
/ /		Death
/ /		Burial

...the spouse of...

139 Name 5X-GRANDMOTHER (FATHER'S SIDE)

DATE	SOURCE	INFORMATION
/ /		Birth
/ /		Baptism
/ /		
/ /		
/ /		
/ /		
/ /		
/ /		
/ /		
/ /		
/ /		
/ /		
/ /		
/ /		
/ /		Death
/ /		Burial

5x-Grandfather (father's side) **Name** **140**

DATE	SOURCE	INFORMATION
/ /		Birth
/ /		Baptism
/ /		
/ /		
/ /		
/ /		
/ /		
/ /		
/ /		
/ /		
/ /		
/ /		
/ /		
/ /		
/ /		Death
/ /		Burial

...the spouse of...

5x-Grandmother (father's side) **Name** **141**

DATE	SOURCE	INFORMATION
/ /		Birth
/ /		Baptism
/ /		
/ /		
/ /		
/ /		
/ /		
/ /		
/ /		
/ /		
/ /		
/ /		
/ /		
/ /		
/ /		Death
/ /		Burial

142 Name 5x-GRANDFATHER (FATHER'S SIDE)

DATE	SOURCE	INFORMATION
/ /		Birth
/ /		Baptism
/ /		
/ /		
/ /		
/ /		
/ /		
/ /		
/ /		
/ /		
/ /		
/ /		
/ /		
/ /		
/ /		Death
/ /		Burial

...the spouse of...

143 Name 5x-GRANDMOTHER (FATHER'S SIDE)

DATE	SOURCE	INFORMATION
/ /		Birth
/ /		Baptism
/ /		
/ /		
/ /		
/ /		
/ /		
/ /		
/ /		
/ /		
/ /		
/ /		
/ /		
/ /		
/ /		Death
/ /		Burial

5x-Grandfather (father's side) **Name** **144**

DATE	SOURCE	INFORMATION
/ /		Birth
/ /		Baptism
/ /		
/ /		
/ /		
/ /		
/ /		
/ /		
/ /		
/ /		
/ /		
/ /		
/ /		
/ /		
/ /		Death
/ /		Burial

...the spouse of...

5x-Grandmother (father's side) **Name** **145**

DATE	SOURCE	INFORMATION
/ /		Birth
/ /		Baptism
/ /		
/ /		
/ /		
/ /		
/ /		
/ /		
/ /		
/ /		
/ /		
/ /		
/ /		
/ /		
/ /		Death
/ /		Burial

146 Name 5X-GRANDFATHER (FATHER'S SIDE)

DATE	SOURCE	INFORMATION
/ /		Birth
/ /		Baptism
/ /		
/ /		
/ /		
/ /		
/ /		
/ /		
/ /		
/ /		
/ /		
/ /		
/ /		
/ /		
/ /		Death
/ /		Burial

...the spouse of...

147 Name 5X-GRANDMOTHER (FATHER'S SIDE)

DATE	SOURCE	INFORMATION
/ /		Birth
/ /		Baptism
/ /		
/ /		
/ /		
/ /		
/ /		
/ /		
/ /		
/ /		
/ /		
/ /		
/ /		
/ /		
/ /		Death
/ /		Burial

5x-GRANDFATHER (FATHER'S SIDE) **Name** **148**

DATE	SOURCE	INFORMATION
/ /		Birth
/ /		Baptism
/ /		
/ /		
/ /		
/ /		
/ /		
/ /		
/ /		
/ /		
/ /		
/ /		
/ /		
/ /		
/ /		Death
/ /		Burial

...the spouse of...

5x-GRANDMOTHER (FATHER'S SIDE) **Name** **149**

DATE	SOURCE	INFORMATION
/ /		Birth
/ /		Baptism
/ /		
/ /		
/ /		
/ /		
/ /		
/ /		
/ /		
/ /		
/ /		
/ /		
/ /		
/ /		
/ /		Death
/ /		Burial

150 Name 5x-GRANDFATHER (FATHER'S SIDE)

DATE	SOURCE	INFORMATION
/ /		Birth
/ /		Baptism
/ /		
/ /		
/ /		
/ /		
/ /		
/ /		
/ /		
/ /		
/ /		
/ /		
/ /		
/ /		
/ /		Death
/ /		Burial

...the spouse of...

151 Name 5x-GRANDMOTHER (FATHER'S SIDE)

DATE	SOURCE	INFORMATION
/ /		Birth
/ /		Baptism
/ /		
/ /		
/ /		
/ /		
/ /		
/ /		
/ /		
/ /		
/ /		
/ /		
/ /		
/ /		
/ /		Death
/ /		Burial

5x-GRANDFATHER (FATHER'S SIDE) **Name** **152**

DATE	SOURCE	INFORMATION
/ /		Birth
/ /		Baptism
/ /		
/ /		
/ /		
/ /		
/ /		
/ /		
/ /		
/ /		
/ /		
/ /		
/ /		
/ /		
/ /		Death
/ /		Burial

...the spouse of...

5x-GRANDMOTHER (FATHER'S SIDE) **Name** **153**

DATE	SOURCE	INFORMATION
/ /		Birth
/ /		Baptism
/ /		
/ /		
/ /		
/ /		
/ /		
/ /		
/ /		
/ /		
/ /		
/ /		
/ /		
/ /		
/ /		Death
/ /		Burial

154 Name

5X-GRANDFATHER (FATHER'S SIDE)

DATE	SOURCE	INFORMATION
/ /		Birth
/ /		Baptism
/ /		
/ /		
/ /		
/ /		
/ /		
/ /		
/ /		
/ /		
/ /		
/ /		
/ /		
/ /		
/ /		Death
/ /		Burial

...the spouse of...

155 Name

5X-GRANDMOTHER (FATHER'S SIDE)

DATE	SOURCE	INFORMATION
/ /		Birth
/ /		Baptism
/ /		
/ /		
/ /		
/ /		
/ /		
/ /		
/ /		
/ /		
/ /		
/ /		
/ /		
/ /		
/ /		Death
/ /		Burial

5X-GRANDFATHER (FATHER'S SIDE) **Name** **156**

DATE	SOURCE	INFORMATION
/ /		Birth
/ /		Baptism
/ /		
/ /		
/ /		
/ /		
/ /		
/ /		
/ /		
/ /		
/ /		
/ /		
/ /		
/ /		
/ /		Death
/ /		Burial

...the spouse of...

5X-GRANDMOTHER (FATHER'S SIDE) **Name** **157**

DATE	SOURCE	INFORMATION
/ /		Birth
/ /		Baptism
/ /		
/ /		
/ /		
/ /		
/ /		
/ /		
/ /		
/ /		
/ /		
/ /		
/ /		
/ /		
/ /		Death
/ /		Burial

158 Name 5x-GRANDFATHER (FATHER'S SIDE)

DATE	SOURCE	INFORMATION
/ /		Birth
/ /		Baptism
/ /		
/ /		
/ /		
/ /		
/ /		
/ /		
/ /		
/ /		
/ /		
/ /		
/ /		
/ /		
/ /		Death
/ /		Burial

...the spouse of...

159 Name 5x-GRANDMOTHER (FATHER'S SIDE)

DATE	SOURCE	INFORMATION
/ /		Birth
/ /		Baptism
/ /		
/ /		
/ /		
/ /		
/ /		
/ /		
/ /		
/ /		
/ /		
/ /		
/ /		
/ /		
/ /		Death
/ /		Burial

5X-GRANDFATHER (FATHER'S SIDE) **Name** **160**

DATE	SOURCE	INFORMATION
/ /		Birth
/ /		Baptism
/ /		
/ /		
/ /		
/ /		
/ /		
/ /		
/ /		
/ /		
/ /		
/ /		
/ /		
/ /		
/ /		Death
/ /		Burial

...the spouse of...

5X-GRANDMOTHER (FATHER'S SIDE) **Name** **161**

DATE	SOURCE	INFORMATION
/ /		Birth
/ /		Baptism
/ /		
/ /		
/ /		
/ /		
/ /		
/ /		
/ /		
/ /		
/ /		
/ /		
/ /		
/ /		
/ /		Death
/ /		Burial

162 Name

5X-GRANDFATHER (FATHER'S SIDE)

DATE	SOURCE	INFORMATION
/ /		Birth
/ /		Baptism
/ /		
/ /		
/ /		
/ /		
/ /		
/ /		
/ /		
/ /		
/ /		
/ /		
/ /		
/ /		
/ /		Death
/ /		Burial

...the spouse of...

163 Name

5X-GRANDMOTHER (FATHER'S SIDE)

DATE	SOURCE	INFORMATION
/ /		Birth
/ /		Baptism
/ /		
/ /		
/ /		
/ /		
/ /		
/ /		
/ /		
/ /		
/ /		
/ /		
/ /		
/ /		
/ /		Death
/ /		Burial

5X-GRANDFATHER (FATHER'S SIDE) **Name** **164**

DATE	SOURCE	INFORMATION
/ /		Birth
/ /		Baptism
/ /		
/ /		
/ /		
/ /		
/ /		
/ /		
/ /		
/ /		
/ /		
/ /		
/ /		
/ /		
/ /		Death
/ /		Burial

...the spouse of...

5X-GRANDMOTHER (FATHER'S SIDE) **Name** **165**

DATE	SOURCE	INFORMATION
/ /		Birth
/ /		Baptism
/ /		
/ /		
/ /		
/ /		
/ /		
/ /		
/ /		
/ /		
/ /		
/ /		
/ /		
/ /		
/ /		Death
/ /		Burial

166 Name

5x-Grandfather (father's side)

DATE	SOURCE	INFORMATION
/ /		Birth
/ /		Baptism
/ /		
/ /		
/ /		
/ /		
/ /		
/ /		
/ /		
/ /		
/ /		
/ /		
/ /		
/ /		
/ /		Death
/ /		Burial

...the spouse of...

167 Name

5x-Grandmother (father's side)

DATE	SOURCE	INFORMATION
/ /		Birth
/ /		Baptism
/ /		
/ /		
/ /		
/ /		
/ /		
/ /		
/ /		
/ /		
/ /		
/ /		
/ /		
/ /		
/ /		Death
/ /		Burial

5X-GRANDFATHER (FATHER'S SIDE) **Name** **168**

DATE	SOURCE	INFORMATION
/ /		Birth
/ /		Baptism
/ /		
/ /		
/ /		
/ /		
/ /		
/ /		
/ /		
/ /		
/ /		
/ /		
/ /		
/ /		
/ /		Death
/ /		Burial

...the spouse of...

5X-GRANDMOTHER (FATHER'S SIDE) **Name** **169**

DATE	SOURCE	INFORMATION
/ /		Birth
/ /		Baptism
/ /		
/ /		
/ /		
/ /		
/ /		
/ /		
/ /		
/ /		
/ /		
/ /		
/ /		
/ /		
/ /		Death
/ /		Burial

170 Name

5X-GRANDFATHER (FATHER'S SIDE)

DATE	SOURCE	INFORMATION
/ /		Birth
/ /		Baptism
/ /		
/ /		
/ /		
/ /		
/ /		
/ /		
/ /		
/ /		
/ /		
/ /		
/ /		
/ /		
/ /		Death
/ /		Burial

...the spouse of...

171 Name

5X-GRANDMOTHER (FATHER'S SIDE)

DATE	SOURCE	INFORMATION
/ /		Birth
/ /		Baptism
/ /		
/ /		
/ /		
/ /		
/ /		
/ /		
/ /		
/ /		
/ /		
/ /		
/ /		
/ /		
/ /		Death
/ /		Burial

5x-GRANDFATHER (FATHER'S SIDE) **Name** **172**

DATE	SOURCE	INFORMATION
/ /		Birth
/ /		Baptism
/ /		
/ /		
/ /		
/ /		
/ /		
/ /		
/ /		
/ /		
/ /		
/ /		
/ /		
/ /		
/ /		Death
/ /		Burial

...the spouse of...

5x-GRANDMOTHER (FATHER'S SIDE) **Name** **173**

DATE	SOURCE	INFORMATION
/ /		Birth
/ /		Baptism
/ /		
/ /		
/ /		
/ /		
/ /		
/ /		
/ /		
/ /		
/ /		
/ /		
/ /		
/ /		
/ /		Death
/ /		Burial

174 Name 5x-Grandfather (father's side)

DATE	SOURCE	INFORMATION
/ /		Birth
/ /		Baptism
/ /		
/ /		
/ /		
/ /		
/ /		
/ /		
/ /		
/ /		
/ /		
/ /		
/ /		
/ /		
/ /		Death
/ /		Burial

...the spouse of...

175 Name 5x-Grandmother (father's side)

DATE	SOURCE	INFORMATION
/ /		Birth
/ /		Baptism
/ /		
/ /		
/ /		
/ /		
/ /		
/ /		
/ /		
/ /		
/ /		
/ /		
/ /		
/ /		
/ /		Death
/ /		Burial

5X-GRANDFATHER (FATHER'S SIDE) **Name**

DATE	SOURCE	INFORMATION
/ /		Birth
/ /		Baptism
/ /		
/ /		
/ /		
/ /		
/ /		
/ /		
/ /		
/ /		
/ /		
/ /		
/ /		
/ /		
/ /		Death
/ /		Burial

...the spouse of...

5X-GRANDMOTHER (FATHER'S SIDE) **Name** **177**

DATE	SOURCE	INFORMATION
/ /		Birth
/ /		Baptism
/ /		
/ /		
/ /		
/ /		
/ /		
/ /		
/ /		
/ /		
/ /		
/ /		
/ /		
/ /		
/ /		Death
/ /		Burial

178 Name 5X-GRANDFATHER (FATHER'S SIDE)

DATE	SOURCE	INFORMATION
/ /		Birth
/ /		Baptism
/ /		
/ /		
/ /		
/ /		
/ /		
/ /		
/ /		
/ /		
/ /		
/ /		
/ /		
/ /		
/ /		Death
/ /		Burial

...the spouse of...

179 Name 5X-GRANDMOTHER (FATHER'S SIDE)

DATE	SOURCE	INFORMATION
/ /		Birth
/ /		Baptism
/ /		
/ /		
/ /		
/ /		
/ /		
/ /		
/ /		
/ /		
/ /		
/ /		
/ /		
/ /		
/ /		Death
/ /		Burial

5X-GRANDFATHER (FATHER'S SIDE) **Name** **180**

DATE	SOURCE	INFORMATION
/ /		Birth
/ /		Baptism
/ /		
/ /		
/ /		
/ /		
/ /		
/ /		
/ /		
/ /		
/ /		
/ /		
/ /		
/ /		
/ /		Death
/ /		Burial

...the spouse of...

5X-GRANDMOTHER (FATHER'S SIDE) **Name** **181**

DATE	SOURCE	INFORMATION
/ /		Birth
/ /		Baptism
/ /		
/ /		
/ /		
/ /		
/ /		
/ /		
/ /		
/ /		
/ /		
/ /		
/ /		
/ /		
/ /		Death
/ /		Burial

182 Name

5x-Grandfather (father's side)

DATE	SOURCE	INFORMATION
/ /		Birth
/ /		Baptism
/ /		
/ /		
/ /		
/ /		
/ /		
/ /		
/ /		
/ /		
/ /		
/ /		
/ /		
/ /		
/ /		Death
/ /		Burial

...the spouse of...

183 Name

5x-Grandmother (father's side)

DATE	SOURCE	INFORMATION
/ /		Birth
/ /		Baptism
/ /		
/ /		
/ /		
/ /		
/ /		
/ /		
/ /		
/ /		
/ /		
/ /		
/ /		
/ /		
/ /		Death
/ /		Burial

5X-GRANDFATHER (FATHER'S SIDE) **Name** **184**

DATE	SOURCE	INFORMATION
/ /		Birth
/ /		Baptism
/ /		
/ /		
/ /		
/ /		
/ /		
/ /		
/ /		
/ /		
/ /		
/ /		
/ /		
/ /		
/ /		Death
/ /		Burial

...the spouse of...

5X-GRANDMOTHER (FATHER'S SIDE) **Name** **185**

DATE	SOURCE	INFORMATION
/ /		Birth
/ /		Baptism
/ /		
/ /		
/ /		
/ /		
/ /		
/ /		
/ /		
/ /		
/ /		
/ /		
/ /		
/ /		
/ /		Death
/ /		Burial

186 Name

5X-GRANDFATHER (FATHER'S SIDE)

DATE	SOURCE	INFORMATION
/ /		Birth
/ /		Baptism
/ /		
/ /		
/ /		
/ /		
/ /		
/ /		
/ /		
/ /		
/ /		
/ /		
/ /		
/ /		
/ /		Death
/ /		Burial

...the spouse of...

187 Name

5X-GRANDMOTHER (FATHER'S SIDE)

DATE	SOURCE	INFORMATION
/ /		Birth
/ /		Baptism
/ /		
/ /		
/ /		
/ /		
/ /		
/ /		
/ /		
/ /		
/ /		
/ /		
/ /		
/ /		
/ /		Death
/ /		Burial

5x-Grandfather (father's side) **Name** **188**

DATE	SOURCE	INFORMATION
/ /		Birth
/ /		Baptism
/ /		
/ /		
/ /		
/ /		
/ /		
/ /		
/ /		
/ /		
/ /		
/ /		
/ /		
/ /		
/ /		Death
/ /		Burial

...the spouse of...

5x-Grandmother (father's side) **Name** **189**

DATE	SOURCE	INFORMATION
/ /		Birth
/ /		Baptism
/ /		
/ /		
/ /		
/ /		
/ /		
/ /		
/ /		
/ /		
/ /		
/ /		
/ /		
/ /		
/ /		Death
/ /		Burial

190 Name

5x-Grandfather (father's side)

DATE	SOURCE	INFORMATION
/ /		Birth
/ /		Baptism
/ /		
/ /		
/ /		
/ /		
/ /		
/ /		
/ /		
/ /		
/ /		
/ /		
/ /		
/ /		
/ /		Death
/ /		Burial

...the spouse of...

191 Name

5x-Grandmother (father's side)

DATE	SOURCE	INFORMATION
/ /		Birth
/ /		Baptism
/ /		
/ /		
/ /		
/ /		
/ /		
/ /		
/ /		
/ /		
/ /		
/ /		
/ /		
/ /		
/ /		Death
/ /		Burial

5X-GRANDFATHER (MOTHER'S SIDE) **Name** **192**

DATE	SOURCE	INFORMATION
/ /		Birth
/ /		Baptism
/ /		
/ /		
/ /		
/ /		
/ /		
/ /		
/ /		
/ /		
/ /		
/ /		
/ /		
/ /		
/ /		Death
/ /		Burial

...the spouse of...

5X-GRANDMOTHER (MOTHER'S SIDE) **Name** **193**

DATE	SOURCE	INFORMATION
/ /		Birth
/ /		Baptism
/ /		
/ /		
/ /		
/ /		
/ /		
/ /		
/ /		
/ /		
/ /		
/ /		
/ /		
/ /		
/ /		Death
/ /		Burial

194 Name

5X-GRANDFATHER (MOTHER'S SIDE)

DATE	SOURCE	INFORMATION
/ /		Birth
/ /		Baptism
/ /		
/ /		
/ /		
/ /		
/ /		
/ /		
/ /		
/ /		
/ /		
/ /		
/ /		
/ /		
/ /		Death
/ /		Burial

...the spouse of...

195 Name

5X-GRANDMOTHER (MOTHER'S SIDE)

DATE	SOURCE	INFORMATION
/ /		Birth
/ /		Baptism
/ /		
/ /		
/ /		
/ /		
/ /		
/ /		
/ /		
/ /		
/ /		
/ /		
/ /		
/ /		
/ /		Death
/ /		Burial

5x-Grandfather (mother's side) **Name** **196**

DATE	SOURCE	INFORMATION
/ /		Birth
/ /		Baptism
/ /		
/ /		
/ /		
/ /		
/ /		
/ /		
/ /		
/ /		
/ /		
/ /		
/ /		
/ /		
/ /		Death
/ /		Burial

...the spouse of...

5x-Grandmother (mother's side) **Name** **197**

DATE	SOURCE	INFORMATION
/ /		Birth
/ /		Baptism
/ /		
/ /		
/ /		
/ /		
/ /		
/ /		
/ /		
/ /		
/ /		
/ /		
/ /		
/ /		
/ /		Death
/ /		Burial

198 Name

5X-GRANDFATHER (MOTHER'S SIDE)

DATE	SOURCE	INFORMATION
/ /		Birth
/ /		Baptism
/ /		
/ /		
/ /		
/ /		
/ /		
/ /		
/ /		
/ /		
/ /		
/ /		
/ /		
/ /		
/ /		Death
/ /		Burial

...the spouse of...

199 Name

5X-GRANDMOTHER (MOTHER'S SIDE)

DATE	SOURCE	INFORMATION
/ /		Birth
/ /		Baptism
/ /		
/ /		
/ /		
/ /		
/ /		
/ /		
/ /		
/ /		
/ /		
/ /		
/ /		
/ /		
/ /		Death
/ /		Burial

5X-GRANDFATHER (MOTHER'S SIDE) **Name** **200**

DATE	SOURCE	INFORMATION
/ /		Birth
/ /		Baptism
/ /		
/ /		
/ /		
/ /		
/ /		
/ /		
/ /		
/ /		
/ /		
/ /		
/ /		
/ /		
/ /		Death
/ /		Burial

...the spouse of...

5X-GRANDMOTHER (MOTHER'S SIDE) **Name** **201**

DATE	SOURCE	INFORMATION
/ /		Birth
/ /		Baptism
/ /		
/ /		
/ /		
/ /		
/ /		
/ /		
/ /		
/ /		
/ /		
/ /		
/ /		
/ /		
/ /		Death
/ /		Burial

202 Name

5X-GRANDFATHER (MOTHER'S SIDE)

DATE	SOURCE	INFORMATION
/ /		Birth
/ /		Baptism
/ /		
/ /		
/ /		
/ /		
/ /		
/ /		
/ /		
/ /		
/ /		
/ /		
/ /		
/ /		
/ /		Death
/ /		Burial

...the spouse of...

203 Name

5X-GRANDMOTHER (MOTHER'S SIDE)

DATE	SOURCE	INFORMATION
/ /		Birth
/ /		Baptism
/ /		
/ /		
/ /		
/ /		
/ /		
/ /		
/ /		
/ /		
/ /		
/ /		
/ /		
/ /		
/ /		Death
/ /		Burial

5x-Grandfather (mother's side) **Name** **204**

DATE	SOURCE	INFORMATION
/ /		Birth
/ /		Baptism
/ /		
/ /		
/ /		
/ /		
/ /		
/ /		
/ /		
/ /		
/ /		
/ /		
/ /		
/ /		
/ /		Death
/ /		Burial

...the spouse of...

5x-Grandmother (mother's side) **Name** **205**

DATE	SOURCE	INFORMATION
/ /		Birth
/ /		Baptism
/ /		
/ /		
/ /		
/ /		
/ /		
/ /		
/ /		
/ /		
/ /		
/ /		
/ /		
/ /		
/ /		Death
/ /		Burial

206 Name 5X-GRANDFATHER (MOTHER'S SIDE)

DATE	SOURCE	INFORMATION
/ /		Birth
/ /		Baptism
/ /		
/ /		
/ /		
/ /		
/ /		
/ /		
/ /		
/ /		
/ /		
/ /		
/ /		
/ /		
/ /		Death
/ /		Burial

...the spouse of...

207 Name 5X-GRANDMOTHER (MOTHER'S SIDE)

DATE	SOURCE	INFORMATION
/ /		Birth
/ /		Baptism
/ /		
/ /		
/ /		
/ /		
/ /		
/ /		
/ /		
/ /		
/ /		
/ /		
/ /		
/ /		
/ /		Death
/ /		Burial

5X-GRANDFATHER (MOTHER'S SIDE) **Name** **208**

DATE	SOURCE	INFORMATION
/ /		Birth
/ /		Baptism
/ /		
/ /		
/ /		
/ /		
/ /		
/ /		
/ /		
/ /		
/ /		
/ /		
/ /		
/ /		
/ /		Death
/ /		Burial

...the spouse of...

5X-GRANDMOTHER (MOTHER'S SIDE) **Name** **209**

DATE	SOURCE	INFORMATION
/ /		Birth
/ /		Baptism
/ /		
/ /		
/ /		
/ /		
/ /		
/ /		
/ /		
/ /		
/ /		
/ /		
/ /		
/ /		
/ /		Death
/ /		Burial

210 Name 5X-GRANDFATHER (MOTHER'S SIDE)

DATE	SOURCE	INFORMATION
/ /		Birth
/ /		Baptism
/ /		
/ /		
/ /		
/ /		
/ /		
/ /		
/ /		
/ /		
/ /		
/ /		
/ /		
/ /		
/ /		Death
/ /		Burial

...the spouse of...

211 Name 5X-GRANDMOTHER (MOTHER'S SIDE)

DATE	SOURCE	INFORMATION
/ /		Birth
/ /		Baptism
/ /		
/ /		
/ /		
/ /		
/ /		
/ /		
/ /		
/ /		
/ /		
/ /		
/ /		
/ /		
/ /		Death
/ /		Burial

5x-GRANDFATHER (MOTHER'S SIDE) **Name** **212**

DATE	SOURCE	INFORMATION
/ /		Birth
/ /		Baptism
/ /		
/ /		
/ /		
/ /		
/ /		
/ /		
/ /		
/ /		
/ /		
/ /		
/ /		
/ /		
/ /		Death
/ /		Burial

...the spouse of...

5x-GRANDMOTHER (MOTHER'S SIDE) **Name** **213**

DATE	SOURCE	INFORMATION
/ /		Birth
/ /		Baptism
/ /		
/ /		
/ /		
/ /		
/ /		
/ /		
/ /		
/ /		
/ /		
/ /		
/ /		
/ /		
/ /		Death
/ /		Burial

214 Name 5X-GRANDFATHER (MOTHER'S SIDE)

DATE	SOURCE	INFORMATION
/ /		Birth
/ /		Baptism
/ /		
/ /		
/ /		
/ /		
/ /		
/ /		
/ /		
/ /		
/ /		
/ /		
/ /		
/ /		
/ /		Death
/ /		Burial

...the spouse of...

215 Name 5X-GRANDMOTHER (MOTHER'S SIDE)

DATE	SOURCE	INFORMATION
/ /		Birth
/ /		Baptism
/ /		
/ /		
/ /		
/ /		
/ /		
/ /		
/ /		
/ /		
/ /		
/ /		
/ /		
/ /		
/ /		Death
/ /		Burial

5X-GRANDFATHER (MOTHER'S SIDE) **Name** **216**

DATE	SOURCE	INFORMATION
/ /		Birth
/ /		Baptism
/ /		
/ /		
/ /		
/ /		
/ /		
/ /		
/ /		
/ /		
/ /		
/ /		
/ /		
/ /		
/ /		Death
/ /		Burial

...the spouse of...

5X-GRANDMOTHER (MOTHER'S SIDE) **Name** **217**

DATE	SOURCE	INFORMATION
/ /		Birth
/ /		Baptism
/ /		
/ /		
/ /		
/ /		
/ /		
/ /		
/ /		
/ /		
/ /		
/ /		
/ /		
/ /		
/ /		Death
/ /		Burial

218 Name 5X-GRANDFATHER (MOTHER'S SIDE)

DATE	SOURCE	INFORMATION
/ /		Birth
/ /		Baptism
/ /		
/ /		
/ /		
/ /		
/ /		
/ /		
/ /		
/ /		
/ /		
/ /		
/ /		
/ /		
/ /		Death
/ /		Burial

...the spouse of...

219 Name 5X-GRANDMOTHER (MOTHER'S SIDE)

DATE	SOURCE	INFORMATION
/ /		Birth
/ /		Baptism
/ /		
/ /		
/ /		
/ /		
/ /		
/ /		
/ /		
/ /		
/ /		
/ /		
/ /		
/ /		
/ /		Death
/ /		Burial

5x-Grandfather (mother's side) **Name** **220**

DATE	SOURCE	INFORMATION
/ /		Birth
/ /		Baptism
/ /		
/ /		
/ /		
/ /		
/ /		
/ /		
/ /		
/ /		
/ /		
/ /		
/ /		
/ /		
/ /		Death
/ /		Burial

...the spouse of...

5x-Grandmother (mother's side) **Name** **221**

DATE	SOURCE	INFORMATION
/ /		Birth
/ /		Baptism
/ /		
/ /		
/ /		
/ /		
/ /		
/ /		
/ /		
/ /		
/ /		
/ /		
/ /		
/ /		
/ /		Death
/ /		Burial

222 Name 5X-GRANDFATHER (MOTHER'S SIDE)

DATE	SOURCE	INFORMATION
/ /		Birth
/ /		Baptism
/ /		
/ /		
/ /		
/ /		
/ /		
/ /		
/ /		
/ /		
/ /		
/ /		
/ /		
/ /		
/ /		Death
/ /		Burial

...the spouse of...

223 Name 5X-GRANDMOTHER (MOTHER'S SIDE)

DATE	SOURCE	INFORMATION
/ /		Birth
/ /		Baptism
/ /		
/ /		
/ /		
/ /		
/ /		
/ /		
/ /		
/ /		
/ /		
/ /		
/ /		
/ /		
/ /		Death
/ /		Burial

5X-GRANDFATHER (MOTHER'S SIDE) **Name** **224**

DATE	SOURCE	INFORMATION
/ /		Birth
/ /		Baptism
/ /		
/ /		
/ /		
/ /		
/ /		
/ /		
/ /		
/ /		
/ /		
/ /		
/ /		
/ /		
/ /		Death
/ /		Burial

...the spouse of...

5X-GRANDMOTHER (MOTHER'S SIDE) **Name** **225**

DATE	SOURCE	INFORMATION
/ /		Birth
/ /		Baptism
/ /		
/ /		
/ /		
/ /		
/ /		
/ /		
/ /		
/ /		
/ /		
/ /		
/ /		
/ /		
/ /		Death
/ /		Burial

226 Name 5X-GRANDFATHER (MOTHER'S SIDE)

DATE	SOURCE	INFORMATION
/ /		Birth
/ /		Baptism
/ /		
/ /		
/ /		
/ /		
/ /		
/ /		
/ /		
/ /		
/ /		
/ /		
/ /		
/ /		
/ /		Death
/ /		Burial

...the spouse of...

227 Name 5X-GRANDMOTHER (MOTHER'S SIDE)

DATE	SOURCE	INFORMATION
/ /		Birth
/ /		Baptism
/ /		
/ /		
/ /		
/ /		
/ /		
/ /		
/ /		
/ /		
/ /		
/ /		
/ /		
/ /		
/ /		Death
/ /		Burial

5X-GRANDFATHER (MOTHER'S SIDE) **Name** **228**

DATE	SOURCE	INFORMATION
/ /		Birth
/ /		Baptism
/ /		
/ /		
/ /		
/ /		
/ /		
/ /		
/ /		
/ /		
/ /		
/ /		
/ /		
/ /		
/ /		Death
/ /		Burial

...the spouse of...

5X-GRANDMOTHER (MOTHER'S SIDE) **Name** **229**

DATE	SOURCE	INFORMATION
/ /		Birth
/ /		Baptism
/ /		
/ /		
/ /		
/ /		
/ /		
/ /		
/ /		
/ /		
/ /		
/ /		
/ /		
/ /		
/ /		Death
/ /		Burial

230 Name 5X-GRANDFATHER (MOTHER'S SIDE)

DATE	SOURCE	INFORMATION
/ /		Birth
/ /		Baptism
/ /		
/ /		
/ /		
/ /		
/ /		
/ /		
/ /		
/ /		
/ /		
/ /		
/ /		
/ /		
/ /		Death
/ /		Burial

...the spouse of...

231 Name 5X-GRANDMOTHER (MOTHER'S SIDE)

DATE	SOURCE	INFORMATION
/ /		Birth
/ /		Baptism
/ /		
/ /		
/ /		
/ /		
/ /		
/ /		
/ /		
/ /		
/ /		
/ /		
/ /		
/ /		
/ /		Death
/ /		Burial

5X-GRANDFATHER (MOTHER'S SIDE) **Name** **232**

DATE	SOURCE	INFORMATION
/ /		Birth
/ /		Baptism
/ /		
/ /		
/ /		
/ /		
/ /		
/ /		
/ /		
/ /		
/ /		
/ /		
/ /		
/ /		
/ /		Death
/ /		Burial

...the spouse of...

5X-GRANDMOTHER (MOTHER'S SIDE) **Name** **233**

DATE	SOURCE	INFORMATION
/ /		Birth
/ /		Baptism
/ /		
/ /		
/ /		
/ /		
/ /		
/ /		
/ /		
/ /		
/ /		
/ /		
/ /		
/ /		
/ /		Death
/ /		Burial

234 Name 5X-GRANDFATHER (MOTHER'S SIDE)

DATE	SOURCE	INFORMATION
/ /		Birth
/ /		Baptism
/ /		
/ /		
/ /		
/ /		
/ /		
/ /		
/ /		
/ /		
/ /		
/ /		
/ /		
/ /		
/ /		Death
/ /		Burial

...the spouse of...

235 Name 5X-GRANDMOTHER (MOTHER'S SIDE)

DATE	SOURCE	INFORMATION
/ /		Birth
/ /		Baptism
/ /		
/ /		
/ /		
/ /		
/ /		
/ /		
/ /		
/ /		
/ /		
/ /		
/ /		
/ /		
/ /		Death
/ /		Burial

5X-GRANDFATHER (MOTHER'S SIDE) **Name** **236**

DATE	SOURCE	INFORMATION
/ /		Birth
/ /		Baptism
/ /		
/ /		
/ /		
/ /		
/ /		
/ /		
/ /		
/ /		
/ /		
/ /		
/ /		
/ /		
/ /		Death
/ /		Burial

...the spouse of...

5X-GRANDMOTHER (MOTHER'S SIDE) **Name** **237**

DATE	SOURCE	INFORMATION
/ /		Birth
/ /		Baptism
/ /		
/ /		
/ /		
/ /		
/ /		
/ /		
/ /		
/ /		
/ /		
/ /		
/ /		
/ /		
/ /		Death
/ /		Burial

238 Name

5X-GRANDFATHER (MOTHER'S SIDE)

DATE	SOURCE	INFORMATION
/ /		Birth
/ /		Baptism
/ /		
/ /		
/ /		
/ /		
/ /		
/ /		
/ /		
/ /		
/ /		
/ /		
/ /		
/ /		
/ /		Death
/ /		Burial

...the spouse of...

239 Name

5X-GRANDMOTHER (MOTHER'S SIDE)

DATE	SOURCE	INFORMATION
/ /		Birth
/ /		Baptism
/ /		
/ /		
/ /		
/ /		
/ /		
/ /		
/ /		
/ /		
/ /		
/ /		
/ /		
/ /		
/ /		Death
/ /		Burial

5X-GRANDFATHER (MOTHER'S SIDE) **Name** **240**

DATE	SOURCE	INFORMATION
/ /		Birth
/ /		Baptism
/ /		
/ /		
/ /		
/ /		
/ /		
/ /		
/ /		
/ /		
/ /		
/ /		
/ /		
/ /		
/ /		Death
/ /		Burial

...the spouse of...

5X-GRANDMOTHER (MOTHER'S SIDE) **Name** **241**

DATE	SOURCE	INFORMATION
/ /		Birth
/ /		Baptism
/ /		
/ /		
/ /		
/ /		
/ /		
/ /		
/ /		
/ /		
/ /		
/ /		
/ /		
/ /		
/ /		Death
/ /		Burial

242 Name

5X-GRANDFATHER (MOTHER'S SIDE)

DATE	SOURCE	INFORMATION
/ /		Birth
/ /		Baptism
/ /		
/ /		
/ /		
/ /		
/ /		
/ /		
/ /		
/ /		
/ /		
/ /		
/ /		
/ /		
/ /		Death
/ /		Burial

...the spouse of...

243 Name

5X-GRANDMOTHER (MOTHER'S SIDE)

DATE	SOURCE	INFORMATION
/ /		Birth
/ /		Baptism
/ /		
/ /		
/ /		
/ /		
/ /		
/ /		
/ /		
/ /		
/ /		
/ /		
/ /		
/ /		
/ /		Death
/ /		Burial

5x-Grandfather (mother's side) **Name** **244**

DATE	SOURCE	INFORMATION
/ /		Birth
/ /		Baptism
/ /		
/ /		
/ /		
/ /		
/ /		
/ /		
/ /		
/ /		
/ /		
/ /		
/ /		
/ /		
/ /		Death
/ /		Burial

...the spouse of...

5x-Grandmother (mother's side) **Name** **245**

DATE	SOURCE	INFORMATION
/ /		Birth
/ /		Baptism
/ /		
/ /		
/ /		
/ /		
/ /		
/ /		
/ /		
/ /		
/ /		
/ /		
/ /		
/ /		
/ /		Death
/ /		Burial

246 Name 5X-GRANDFATHER (MOTHER'S SIDE)

DATE	SOURCE	INFORMATION
/ /		Birth
/ /		Baptism
/ /		
/ /		
/ /		
/ /		
/ /		
/ /		
/ /		
/ /		
/ /		
/ /		
/ /		
/ /		
/ /		Death
/ /		Burial

...the spouse of...

247 Name 5X-GRANDMOTHER (MOTHER'S SIDE)

DATE	SOURCE	INFORMATION
/ /		Birth
/ /		Baptism
/ /		
/ /		
/ /		
/ /		
/ /		
/ /		
/ /		
/ /		
/ /		
/ /		
/ /		
/ /		
/ /		Death
/ /		Burial

5X-GRANDFATHER (MOTHER'S SIDE) **Name** **248**

DATE	SOURCE	INFORMATION
/ /		Birth
/ /		Baptism
/ /		
/ /		
/ /		
/ /		
/ /		
/ /		
/ /		
/ /		
/ /		
/ /		
/ /		
/ /		
/ /		Death
/ /		Burial

...the spouse of...

5X-GRANDMOTHER (MOTHER'S SIDE) **Name** **249**

DATE	SOURCE	INFORMATION
/ /		Birth
/ /		Baptism
/ /		
/ /		
/ /		
/ /		
/ /		
/ /		
/ /		
/ /		
/ /		
/ /		
/ /		
/ /		
/ /		Death
/ /		Burial

250 Name

5x-Grandfather (mother's side)

DATE	SOURCE	INFORMATION
/ /		Birth
/ /		Baptism
/ /		
/ /		
/ /		
/ /		
/ /		
/ /		
/ /		
/ /		
/ /		
/ /		
/ /		
/ /		
/ /		Death
/ /		Burial

...the spouse of...

251 Name

5x-Grandmother (mother's side)

DATE	SOURCE	INFORMATION
/ /		Birth
/ /		Baptism
/ /		
/ /		
/ /		
/ /		
/ /		
/ /		
/ /		
/ /		
/ /		
/ /		
/ /		
/ /		
/ /		Death
/ /		Burial

5X-GRANDFATHER (MOTHER'S SIDE) **Name** **252**

DATE	SOURCE	INFORMATION
/ /		Birth
/ /		Baptism
/ /		
/ /		
/ /		
/ /		
/ /		
/ /		
/ /		
/ /		
/ /		
/ /		
/ /		
/ /		
/ /		Death
/ /		Burial

...the spouse of...

5X-GRANDMOTHER (MOTHER'S SIDE) **Name** **253**

DATE	SOURCE	INFORMATION
/ /		Birth
/ /		Baptism
/ /		
/ /		
/ /		
/ /		
/ /		
/ /		
/ /		
/ /		
/ /		
/ /		
/ /		
/ /		
/ /		Death
/ /		Burial

254 Name 5x-GRANDFATHER (MOTHER'S SIDE)

DATE	SOURCE	INFORMATION
/ /		Birth
/ /		Baptism
/ /		
/ /		
/ /		
/ /		
/ /		
/ /		
/ /		
/ /		
/ /		
/ /		
/ /		
/ /		
/ /		Death
/ /		Burial

...the spouse of...

255 Name 5x-GRANDMOTHER (MOTHER'S SIDE)

DATE	SOURCE	INFORMATION
/ /		Birth
/ /		Baptism
/ /		
/ /		
/ /		
/ /		
/ /		
/ /		
/ /		
/ /		
/ /		
/ /		
/ /		
/ /		
/ /		Death
/ /		Burial

COUSIN RELATIONSHIP CALCULATOR

To find the relationship between two relatives, find a common ancestor between them. Look for the relationship that ancestor is to the first person along the top. Then look for the relationship the same ancestor is to the other person down the side. Where the two meet gives the relationship. So, for example, if your grandparent was your relative's great-grandparent, that means you are your relative are 1st cousins once removed.

You Your cousin	PARENT	GRANDPARENT	GREAT-GRANDPARENT	2x-GREAT-GRANDPARENT	3x-GREAT-GRANDPARENT	4x-GREAT-GRANDPARENT	5x-GREAT-GRANDPARENT
PARENT	Siblings	Niece/nephew	Great niece/nephew	2x great niece/nephew	3x great niece/nephew	4x great niece/nephew	5x great niece/nephew
GRANDPARENT	Uncle/aunt	1st cousins	1st cousins once removed	1st cousins twice removed	1st cousins 3 times removed	1st cousins 4 times removed	1st cousins 5 times removed
GREAT-GRANDPARENT	Great uncle/ great aunt	1st cousins once removed	2nd cousins	2nd cousins 1 time removed	2nd cousins 2 times removed	2nd cousins 3 times removed	2nd cousins 4 times removed
2x-GREAT-GRANDPARENT	2x great uncle/ 2x great aunt	1st cousins twice removed	2nd cousins 1 time removed	3rd cousins	3rd cousins 1 time removed	3rd cousins 2 times removed	3rd cousins 3 times removed
3x-GREAT-GRANDPARENT	3x great uncle/ 3x great aunt	1st cousins 3 times removed	2nd cousins 2 times removed	3rd cousins 1 time removed	4th cousins	4th cousins 1 time removed	4th cousins 2 times removed
4x-GREAT-GRANDPARENT	4x great uncle/ 4x great aunt	1st cousins 4 times removed	2nd cousins 3 times removed	3rd cousins 2 times removed	4th cousins 1 time removed	5th cousins	5th cousins 1 time removed
5x-GREAT-GRANDPARENT	5x great uncle/ 5x great aunt	1st cousins 5 times removed	2nd cousins 4 times removed	3rd cousins 3 times removed	4th cousins 2 times removed	5th cousins 1 time removed	6th cousins

FAMILY HISTORY RECORD TIMELINE

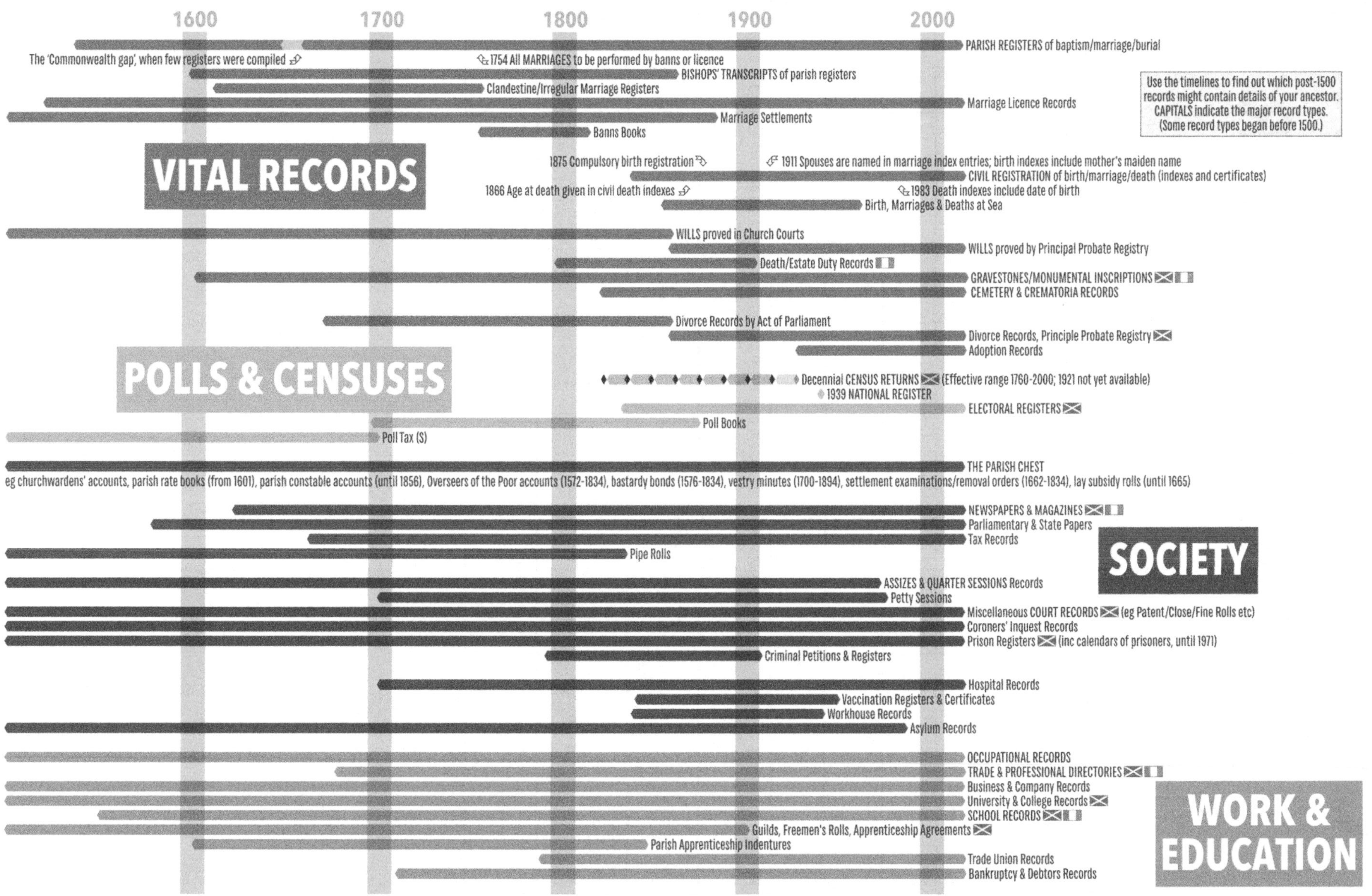

1600
1700
1800
1900
2000
PARISH REGISTERS of baptism/marriage/burial
The 'Commonwealth gap', when few registers were compiled
1754 All MARRIAGES to be performed by banns or licence
BISHOPS' TRANSCRIPTS of parish registers
Clandestine/Irregular Marriage Registers
Marriage Licence Records
Marriage Settlements
Banns Books
Use the timelines to find out which post-1500 records might contain details of your ancestor. CAPITALS indicate the major record types. (Some record types began before 1500.)
VITAL RECORDS
1875 Compulsory birth registration
1911 Spouses are named in marriage index entries; birth indexes include mother's maiden name
CIVIL REGISTRATION of birth/marriage/death (indexes and certificates)
1866 Age at death given in civil death indexes
1983 Death indexes include date of birth
Birth, Marriages & Deaths at Sea
WILLS proved in Church Courts
WILLS proved by Principal Probate Registry
Death/Estate Duty Records
GRAVESTONES/MONUMENTAL INSCRIPTIONS
CEMETERY & CREMATORIA RECORDS
Divorce Records by Act of Parliament
Divorce Records, Principle Probate Registry
Adoption Records
POLLS & CENSUSES
Decennial CENSUS RETURNS (Effective range 1760-2000; 1921 not yet available)
1939 NATIONAL REGISTER
ELECTORAL REGISTERS
Poll Books
Poll Tax (S)
THE PARISH CHEST
eg churchwardens' accounts, parish rate books (from 1601), parish constable accounts (until 1856), Overseers of the Poor accounts (1572-1834), bastardy bonds (1576-1834), vestry minutes (1700-1894), settlement examinations/removal orders (1662-1834), lay subsidy rolls (until 1665)
NEWSPAPERS & MAGAZINES
Parliamentary & State Papers
Tax Records
SOCIETY
Pipe Rolls
ASSIZES & QUARTER SESSIONS Records
Petty Sessions
Miscellaneous COURT RECORDS (eg Patent/Close/Fine Rolls etc)
Coroners' Inquest Records
Prison Registers (inc calendars of prisoners, until 1971)
Criminal Petitions & Registers
Hospital Records
Vaccination Registers & Certificates
Workhouse Records
Asylum Records
OCCUPATIONAL RECORDS
TRADE & PROFESSIONAL DIRECTORIES
Business & Company Records
University & College Records
SCHOOL RECORDS
Guilds, Freemen's Rolls, Apprenticeship Agreements
Parish Apprenticeship Indentures
Trade Union Records
Bankruptcy & Debtors Records
WORK & EDUCATION

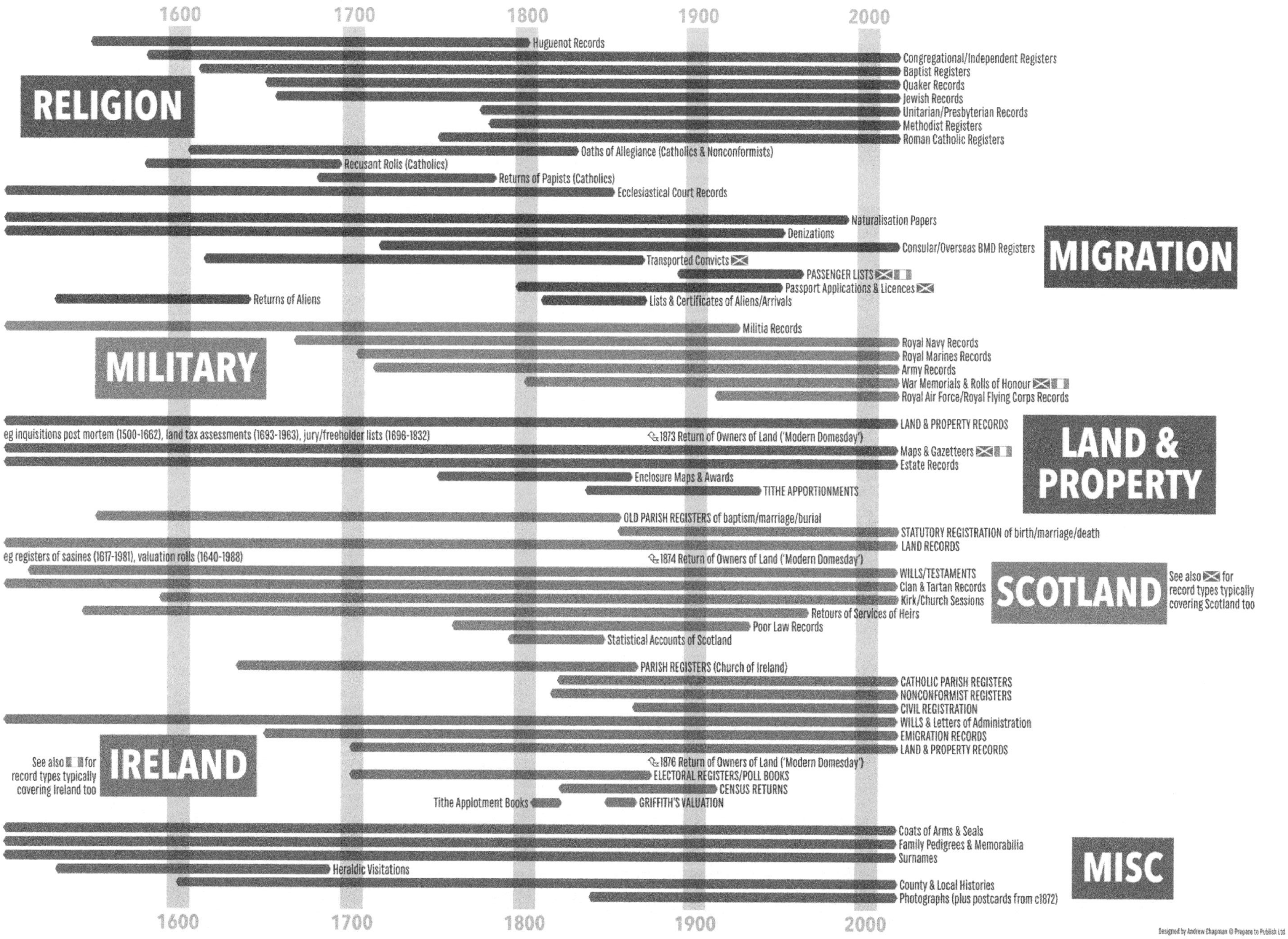

1600
1700
1800
1900
2000
RELIGION
Huguenot Records
Congregational/Independent Registers
Baptist Registers
Quaker Records
Jewish Records
Unitarian/Presbyterian Records
Methodist Registers
Roman Catholic Registers
Oaths of Allegiance (Catholics & Nonconformists)
Recusant Rolls (Catholics)
Returns of Papists (Catholics)
Ecclesiastical Court Records
MIGRATION
Naturalisation Papers
Denizations
Consular/Overseas BMD Registers
Transported Convicts
PASSENGER LISTS
Passport Applications & Licences
Returns of Aliens
Lists & Certificates of Aliens/Arrivals
MILITARY
Militia Records
Royal Navy Records
Royal Marines Records
Army Records
War Memorials & Rolls of Honour
Royal Air Force/Royal Flying Corps Records
LAND & PROPERTY
LAND & PROPERTY RECORDS
eg inquisitions post mortem (1500-1662), land tax assessments (1693-1963), jury/freeholder lists (1696-1832)
1873 Return of Owners of Land ('Modern Domesday')
Maps & Gazetteers
Estate Records
Enclosure Maps & Awards
TITHE APPORTIONMENTS
SCOTLAND
OLD PARISH REGISTERS of baptism/marriage/burial
STATUTORY REGISTRATION of birth/marriage/death
LAND RECORDS
eg registers of sasines (1617-1981), valuation rolls (1640-1988)
1874 Return of Owners of Land ('Modern Domesday')
WILLS/TESTAMENTS
Clan & Tartan Records
Kirk/Church Sessions
Retours of Services of Heirs
Poor Law Records
Statistical Accounts of Scotland
See also for record types typically covering Scotland too
IRELAND
PARISH REGISTERS (Church of Ireland)
CATHOLIC PARISH REGISTERS
NONCONFORMIST REGISTERS
CIVIL REGISTRATION
WILLS & Letters of Administration
EMIGRATION RECORDS
LAND & PROPERTY RECORDS
1876 Return of Owners of Land ('Modern Domesday')
ELECTORAL REGISTERS/POLL BOOKS
CENSUS RETURNS
Tithe Applotment Books
GRIFFITH'S VALUATION
See also for record types typically covering Ireland too
MISC
Coats of Arms & Seals
Family Pedigrees & Memorabilia
Surnames
Heraldic Visitations
County & Local Histories
Photographs (plus postcards from c1872)
Designed by Andrew Chapman © Prepare to Publish Ltd

Made in the USA
Monee, IL
01 April 2022

93923746R00085